"The country must forge ahead with a higher rate of economic growth, but that growth process must generate more employment, must be equitable, socially just and humane. Agriculture and our farmers must receive more focused attention. India must shine for the poor, it must shine for the Scheduled Castes, Scheduled Tribes, other backward classes and Minorities. India must shine in the cities and the villages. We want India to shine, and shine for all."

— Dr. Manmohan Singh
at his first press conference
as Prime Minister, September 04, 2004

MANMOHAN'S DREAM INDIA

His Vision of Growth, Equity and Social Change vis-a-vis Economic Reforms

MANMOHAN'S DREAM INDIA

His Vision of Growth, Equity and Social Change vis-a-vis Economic Reforms

V.S. MAHAJAN
Director, Centre for Indian Development Studies, Chandigarh

DEEP & DEEP PUBLICATIONS PVT. LTD.
F-159, Rajouri Garden, New Delhi - 110 027

MANMOHAN'S DREAM INDIA

ISBN 81-7629-631-7

Printed in India at MAYUR ENTERPRISES,
WZ Plot No. 3, Gujjar Market, Tihar Village, New Delhi - 110 018.

Published by DEEP & DEEP PUBLICATIONS PVT. LTD.,
F-159, Rajouri Garden, New Delhi - 110 027 • Phone : 25435369, 25440916
E-mail : deep98@del3.vsnl.net.in • ddpbooks@yahoo.co.in
Showroom :
2/13, Ansari Road, Daryaganj, New Delhi - 110 002 • Telefax : 23245122

Dedicated to the
poor whose development
is the basic goal of the
present UPA Government

Contents

Introduction

'Manmohan' sounds a refreshing name. Even more refreshing is his careergraph whether as a student, or a teacher, or a UN expert, or a civil servant, or a finance minister, and now Prime Minister. In fact everywhere he has left his mark of high quality.

The last I wrote on Manmohan Singh was in 1995 when he was the finance minister and the book was titled 'Manmohan's India'. Since then the situation has changed a lot.

As a finance minister his concern was to rescue the highly disturbed economy in the country when it barely had a few days foreign exchange to finance its trade. His sharp mind had perceived that the only feasible solution under the circumstances was to free the country from its bureaucratic controlled system and turn it into a global economy with free trade and open market.

His bold attempt was met with high opposition and it were the communists who opposed it vehemently. But then with the strong support of his Prime Minister Narasimha Rao he had his way. Soon even the staunch opponents had also realised that the country needed this bold strategy if its economy were to be put on the fast track of growth.

By the time he had left in 1996, after the Congress defeat in the elections, the country was fast growing with large inflow of foreign investment and technology both in consumer and capital industries as well as services. All the subsequent governments that ruled the country never disturbed the open economy model. Rather even tried to strengthen it further and the maximum support came from the BJP-led Government which lasted for full five years.

But then after the gap of eight years when the Congress was again voted to power it was realised that the ground realities had meanwhile considerably changed. The country's excessive reliance on the open economy had failed to benefit the rural areas. There was thus lop-sided growth with distance between rural and urban development having fast widened. In fact, a large share of benefits from globalization had been pocketed by the urban areas leaving the rural areas far behind. Poverty had enormously risen in villages and so did unemployment.

In fact with little development occurring in rural areas, a large number of young people from these areas have migrated to the urban areas in search for green pastures but are hardly successful. Now the vast gap that has resulted by excessive concentration on urban development is being sought to be rectified.

There is little doubt that Manmohan Singh with his vision, commitment and dedication would succeed in this Herculean task, as he has done in the past. The country can rely on him in bringing about Second Revolution this time in the rural areas—while earlier it has been in the urban areas. Thus, balance between the two sectors so essential for the overall development in the country, is now being sought to be achieved.

This book therefore tries to look closely into the agenda of Manmohan Singh's government for transference of the Indian economy into a new look rural development and bring it at par with urban development. This I call 'Second Revolution' after the 'First Revolution'. Both revolutions together would complete the cycle of total transformation of this country's economy and prepare it for a more secure and stable economy to take the full advantage of global economy. Undoubtedly if we are able to achieve successfully the 'Second Revolution' the country would be a major front runner in the global economy, which was very much the earnest dream of Rajiv Gandhi and which it is very much hoped Manmohan Singh would complete now.

In writing this book the help rendered by Mr. G.S. Bhatia of Deep and Deep Publications (P) Ltd. is to be acknowledged. He also ensured that the book was published in a record time.

Chandigarh V.S. MAHAJAN

1

Development of India : Looking at the Recent Past

Interestingly it was during the earlier period of Rajiv's governance in the mid-1980s that he showed great interest in India's modernisation and would have brought the country on global level had his zeal not slowed down during the later period on the advise of his inner group who were worried that this approach would not be acceptable to the country when elections were around and would definitely result in a major defeat for the Congress. And this also convinced Rajiv. He had thus made a dramatic change in his strategy of country's development and came down heavily on the introduction of poverty-alleviation programmes to encourage overall rural development.

Even in planning he introduced the concept of decentralisation in a big way and district became the centre for planning. All this is obvious from the reproduction of material from the earlier book 'Manmohan's India and Other Current Writings'—henceforth called : 'Manmohan's India' (Deep and Deep Publications Pvt. Ltd., New Delhi, 1994) :

"While often we have talked about Rajiv's India for he happened to be a great champion of liberalisation and modernisation of this country's political and economic structure in order that when it entered the next century it was at par with world's top countries. Unfortunately his dream has remained unrealised. During the closing years of his office he had, mostly because of political compulsions, dramatically shifted the whole strategy towards rural development where a host of schemes and programmes for the poor were rushed through. In fact, Rajiv Gandhi had shown unusual interest in areas like decentralised planning and mass poverty alleviation programmes. The latter were tackled in a big way through massive investment of Jawahar Rozgar Yojana—the biggest ever programme for rural job creation. In this process he had moved far way from his earlier zeal of total modernisation of India industrial economy and the service sector. Despite such dramatic change he had however failed, rather miserably, to lead his party to victory in the next election. Perhaps it was due to the fact that his new policy of rural transformation, which though was close to reality, had been tried rather late and it was as well far too a short period to bring about any dramatic results.

"It was only after nearly 20 months of Rajiv's exit that we find Dr. Manmohan Singh, the new finance minister, emerging on the scene and very much trying to complete the task of liberalisation and modernisation of India's economy left half-complete by Rajiv. Unlike Rajiv, Manmohan however is under heavy pressure by the World Bank to complete this task as quickly as possible. And Manmohan, a true loyalist, does not want to let down the World Bank for the latter's generosity in sanctioning big loans, particularly at a time when the country was passing through one of the worst financial crisis. Whether this task of setting the domestic economy in better health as well improving the foreign exchange position could not have been approached through alternative and perhaps more honourable ways is of course a different thing. In any case, it is the total love for liberalisation that is uppermost in their mind.

"It is therefore logical to conclude that Rajiv's India has now passed on to Manmohan and the task of taking the country to the 21st century now appears to be Manmohan's concern."

A little further in Section 2 of this book we find reasons why Rajiv's policy of rural development had failed to work :

"In 1989 as election strategy, Rajiv's government had announced a package of liberal economic programmes mainly to win over the sympathies of the downtrodden members of the society. Surprisingly during the first three and a half years of his term the Prime Minister had been selling his programme of ultra-modernisation where high emphasis was laid on latest technology and over-liberalisation of import policies to allow foreign technocrats and their technologies to have an easy access into the country. In fact, there was all along mention of Rajiv's New India which while enter the 21st century would be fully loaded with electronics, computers, various consumer gadgets what not there would be all around the aroma of complete modernisation. Further to achieve this end the Prime Minister had encouraged a large number of high fund consuming programmes and studies, practically touching every area of the economy, to ensure India's safe entry into the next century where it would be enjoying status close with the top countries in the world.

"And for undertaking these studies at a short notice and in the absence of appropriate data, all norms of financial and organisational constraints were thrown into wind. The result was that the exchequer had to shell out big sums at short notices. While these committees created in hurry were not well equipped to undertake such task, there occurred haphazard expansion of the personnel most of whom were misfits. All this only resulted in huge wastage of public funds and hardly anything concrete emerged from such high-tech exercises. No surprise that most of these half-baked reports, prepared without lack of direction are now gathering dust in the basements of government offices. Not only such exercise on futurology has proved futile, the high dose of money pumped recklessly into these committees only helped to fuel inflation.

"That was the way the country had proceeded upto the middle of 1988. Subsequently, there was a sudden change in the strategy of our Prime Minister. Naturally with elections not far away, his close advisers had brought to his notice the urgent need for highlighting those programmes which touched the masses as ultimately in the Indian democracy it were the rural people who decided the fate of the country. Thus, it was basically the question of mere numbers where the rural masses predominated. Thus, they had to be won over with programmes that directly touched them.

"There was therefore sudden reversal of the whole strategy of Mr. Rajiv Gandhi. Instead of highlighting in his speeches and programmes about taking India into the 21st century as a fully modernised country, now he began to emphasis on the programmes to help rural transformation. This was very much evident in his Independence day speech of 1988 and even more so of 1989 where every possible emphasis was laid on new programmes introduced for rural development.

"But then these programmes are prepared in equal hurry like the earlier ones. They are equally half-bake, lack thrust and direction. They thus sound mere gimmicks to the rural poor to win over their sympathies in the coming election. When we have a close look at the spate of programmes like decentralised planning, Panchayati Raj and Jawahar Rozgar Yojana these do not carry much conviction under the prevailing conditions. Rather the way these have been prepared and are to be executed, there is very likelihood that these would result in frittering away country's resources in rich abundance without achieving the much projected effects.

"Take the instance of decentralised planning. It is of course not a new concept. It has been very much there right from the Nehru era. In fact, the whole programme of Community Development introduced in the early fifties was basically to lay the foundations of such grassroot planning. Then what happened? The magic of community development as well as of Panchayati Raj and building cooperative rural development societies—soon waned away. In fact, Mr. S.K. Dey, who was the architect of community development programme, was both the first and last Minister of Community Development and Panchayati Raj in Nehru's cabinet. There has been no such Ministry subsequently. Both the programmes of decentralised development and Panchayati Raj have been lying low since. And now suddenly after couple of decades, awareness has again dawned to rejuvenate them without first understanding and going deep into the factors that had led to their long failure.

"Now the structuring of the Eighth Plan basically depends on the flow of data from the district level. It is a good idea but then can it be done in a short period and without weighing the colossal cost factor? Already the State Planning Boards are in a bad shape and have turned into hotbeds of politics and corruption. As a matter of fact had these bodies been properly guided and administered these should have helped in gathering the needed information at district level. But then they were hardly interested in undertaking such a task. How could then the Planning Commission go about in completing this gigantic task, with so many constraints, where couple of hundreds of districts are involved? No surprise the Eighth Plan has already been unnecessarily delayed and now with the elections around one does know its final fate.

"Next take the case of Panchayati Raj. It has already run into rough weather and how it looks that the task of changing the Constitution to accommodate the Centre's new approach toward the functioning of panchayats would be put into cold storage. It again shows that this measure was drafted in great hurry without first understanding the pulse of the country.

"And then there is Jawahar Rozgar Yojana. There are already several rural development programmes, capped by the long-time Integrated Rural Development Programme, which have failed to take-off. As a matter of fact already several hundred crores of rupees have been sunk in the rural sector in the name of these programmes and yet the percentage of population below the poverty line instead of declining has been rising. Obviously large funds that have gone into programmes, instead of benefiting those for whom meant, have actually disappeared into the pockets of administrators, politicians and middlemen. This has been again another factor fuelling inflation in the country and adding to its stock of black money.

"Under the circumstances it is idle to expect Jawahar Rozgar Yojana to work miracles. Rather it would further encourage the demon of inflation and there is very little likelihood that the beneficiary from the programme would be the rural poor. Much of these funds, as the experience shows, would be cornered by those very people who administer these funds as well as the politicians. Thus, only a small amount will ultimately reach the real beneficiaries.

"And now the Prime Minister has come out with his latest gimmick of announcing rise in the procurement prices of almost all agricultural commodities without appreciating the adverse consequences of such a move. It will further add to the inflationary spiral in the country.

"To sum up one notices that without proper thinking, planning and direction several earlier programmes in the name of instant modernisation of the economy and recently to uplift the rural masses almost overnight from their age-old poverty and other problems, have been started. Naturally the end result could not be other than further widening the income distribution pattern as well as quickening inflationary spiral."

CHANGE OF GOVERNMENT AT THE CENTRE

In 1989 when V.P. Singh's government was voted into power—V.P. was earlier finance minister in Rajiv's government and later defence minister—we find that the country faced a period of high uncertainty, turmoil, economic instability; and after him there were frequent changes in leadership when we had two short-time prime minister in Charan Singh and Chandra Shekhar. They made the country's political and economic situation still worse.

Thus in 1991 when the new government of Congress was again voted into power the country's economy had been completely shattered and it had to go in for a massive loan from the World Bank to bail out the economy from its high debt situation and put it on the rails. Before the loan was sanctioned the World Bank put conditionalities like reversal of the current highly bureaucratic hindrances in the free flow of foreign trade, investments and technology and thus the country was asked to ensure freedom in all these areas.

The Bank also virtually suggested the name of Manmohan Singh to undertake this arduous task. That's how Manmohan became the country's finance minister. He undertook this difficult task of bringing back economic stability in the country through the implementation of programmes of liberalisation and globalisation with success. In fact, within a record time he changed the whole history of economic development in the country.

We here again reproduce from 'Manmohan's India' (pp. 17-20) :

"Now when one looks back and does a stock-taking of the economy there are certainly encouraging signs of recovery though not to the extent that even Manmohan had hoped. But then it was very well-known that prolonged damage caused under the previous regimes of V.P. Singh and to some extent of Chandra Shekhar could not be set right so easily.

Long-term Growth

"It is well-known that for long-term growth there are certain well-recognised norms. One of these is political stability without which it is very difficult to make business decisions. Industrialists are not so much bothered with short-term stability as with long-term. Experience shows that countries which have made rapid progress have also maintained long-term political stability. It is quite obvious from the study of either Japan or Germany, the two international giants which have emerged almost from the ashes.

"Simultaneously with political stability there is the key role played by the correct economic policies pursued by the government. Here again the experience of both Japan and Germany as well of other fast growing economies, like South Korea and Singapore in Asia, show special care had been taken by their governments to encourage healthy growth of private capitalism. As a matter of fact government policies were so built and used as to promote high industrial growth and not to become obstacles. In other words, liberal but well considered state policies have yielded remarkable results. Thus, all the above mentioned countries are enjoying high growth rates in income, employment, saving, investment and output. And yet these economies have faced remarkably low rates of inflation. In fact, their growth rates have risen much faster than either wages or prices.

"Another equally important element in the growth process, is that these countries have successfully created a class of highly disciplined and conscientious workforce. These workers are hardworking, dedicated and eager to contribute to higher production where liberal incentives are offered. Thus committed working class, dedicated to the country, is an important force behind sustained industrial growth. While it might be easier to build the outfit of industry by importing latest plant and equipment from foreign countries, it is tough job to create a class of disciplined labour. Singapore's example shows how this small island country has come to occupy a significant place in industry and trade when just couple of decades ago it was like any backward economy. This miracle has been achieved by the united effort of a progressive and watchful government as well committed labour force conscious of discipline, productivity and competition.

Multiple Controls

"I have intentionally dealt with the above in order to appreciate our own growth process. While this country had enjoyed a long spell of political stability after independence, barring short period of disturbances, we did not have until recently a dynamic industrial policy. Rather we had shot our economy under a system of multiple controls, where highly complicated and ambiguous rules and regulations far more encouraged corruption, redtapism and delays than serve their real purpose. And very unfortunately this process was made further tight as the time passed and thus we failed to cash this political stability for promoting high and sustained industrial growth.

"Further, while the country has highly protective legislation for labour, it has hardly tried to discipline the labour force which could have instilled in them a sense of commitment and dedication. How things have gone wrong with our labour force are obvious from the experience of our public sector giants which the politicians are fond of labelling "the commanding heights" mainly to win political support. There has been phenomenal growth of these units after independence, thanks to our misplaced socialistic commitments. This is a sector which has encouraged ill-disciplined and pampered class of workers where most shirk work, as a matter of fact hardly have any interest in what they are expected to do, while away their time in union activities and absent when find opportunity. The story is the same in all public sector units.

"So with such atmosphere how could one expect a sense of commitment and dedication from these workers, who as well enjoy high wages, DAs and several facilities, which in no way bear relationship to their work culture and productivity. No surprise most public units, despite going in for latest technology and several other facilities at the cost of the exchequer, have failed to take-off and several of them continue to be in the red even after several years of establishment.

"Thus the lesson is quite clear. Unless this country creates a class of disciplined labour force, it would be difficult to reach the goal of high industrial growth. Here a lot is going to depend on our administration and its labour policies which should be progressive, forward-looking and in tune with the changing times, particularly there should be special rewards and incentives for those workers who show initiative and put up good results and the same time punishment for those who neglect their duties. Also laws regarding unions need to be properly framed so that these unions become result-oriented. In fact, these can play an important role in bringing about a sense of discipline and work culture among their members.

"It is in this context that disinvestment in the public sector would be appreciated. More funds, thus available, could be invested in other far more important areas, particularly in improving services that play vital role in industrial growth itself.

Inflation

"It is heartening to find that the rate of inflation has steadily moved from two digit to single unit. The situation is likely to improve further. Its rise after the present government took over was natural because the whole mechanism of promoting growth through new investment and structural reforms as well creating confidence among foreign business houses needed time. All these efforts are now slowly yielding results and prices are as well getting disciplined. As mentioned earlier, those countries which have risen fast in their growth have also shown slow rise in their inflation rates. The same could happen here if we succeed in our industrial growth strategy which would automatically take care of both wages and prices."

OVERALL SITUATION

Overall, during the past two decades the country has passed through several stages of development—initially it was Rajiv's liberalisation and modernisation approach which was subsequently changed into the strategy of poverty-alleviation, rural development and decentralised planning.

Then followed highly unstable situation for couple of years resulting in colossal damage to the country's economy causing heavy accumulation of foreign debt and poor stage of country's foreign exchange situation. It was only after the return of Congress government that stable situation emerged again in the country.

This era had also laid down a firm regime of globalisation and open market economy which has contributed substantially to strengthening the country's weak economy. However, at the same time gains from such approach have by and large concentrated in urban areas, the rural areas have failed to get even a fraction of these benefits. In fact, the recent growth has left behind a wide gap between rural and urban development.

In consequence, there has been a large growth of poverty and unemployment in rural areas. Early correction of such lop-sided growth has been one of the principal factors behind the recent failure of the BJP-led government.

2

Manmohan's Careergraph : A Unique Experience

Manmohan has been a brilliant student. Born on September 26, 1932 at Gah (West Pakistan), he was educated at Universities of Panjab, Cambridge and Oxford. After his creditable performance in MA Economics from the Panjab University where he stood first, he was sent for higher studies at the Oxford University at the university expenses. At Oxford he showed his brilliant performance again and secured the degree with honour. On return, he joined the Panjab University as a Lecturer in Economics and soon was promoted as a Reader.

After a gap, he again joined the Oxford University for doctorate and secured D. Phil. degree and subsequently earned D. Litt. (Honoris Causa) degree. He was the youngest professor at the Panjab University.

When I joined the Panjab University in 1964 he was very much there and led a very active and busy academic life. He was a very popular teacher. His lectures were well-attended. Students would not like to miss them. Even at a young age he was also popular with the government and his advise and guidance was often sought in issues pertaining his interest.

It was on one of such occasions that I had the privilege to accompany him on a tour of border districts where he was commissioned by the Punjab Government to make on the spot assessment of the loss suffered by industries in border towns as a consequence of Indo-Pak war in 1965 and give his recommendations about the help that should be provided.

During this tour Manmohan took me along with him. The government had provided the vehicle. It was a good opportunity for me to know this gentleman from a close angle.

He told me he would pick me up from my residence at a particular time. He was there and had to wait in the verandha of our house when I took little longer to get ready. He waited patiently. We got together on the back seats of the car and during journey discussed several issues pertaining to planning and Punjab economy. He was quick-witted and we often entered into a lively debate. He would often doze off during the journey and seemed to enjoy these occasional breaks.

We first visited Batala which was a foundry business centre with a large number of engineering units. The industrialists of that place were already waiting for us. Without wasting time Manmohan went straight to the business and through a lengthy talk with them acquired himself with their problems and developed a rough a lengthy talk with them acquired himself with their problems and developed a rough strategy to help them. Copious notes were taken on the occasion where I helped him, besides gaining my own insight into the peculiar border problems.

Next we had moved to Amritsar where again a large number of !ocal businessmen were waiting at the appointed place and again unmindful of the pressure that this hectic tour had imposed on us, Manmohan first of all expressed his regret for keeping them waiting for reasons beyond him control. Again there were several complaints and several notes were taken by both of us. By now more light had been thrown on the strategy that border towns needed for protecting them against their vulnerability to frequent attacks from across the border.

We stayed for the night in Amritsar. Manmohan dropped me at the place I was to stay with my cousin and before leaving told me the time he would pick me up the next morning for our visit to Jalandhar and Ludhiana—the two mega industrial towns equally affected by the war—before we finally returned to Chandigarh.

He was again punctual to the time and this time was more careful not to let Manmohan wait, though he spent time talking with my cousin and when he learnt that he was a Branch Manager of the L.I.C. added his brother-in-law was also a Branch Manager of L.I.C.

There was the usual crowd of industrialists waiting in Jalandhar. They had prepared a long list of grievances and wanted urgent help from the Government in case the industry was to survive in border areas. This time mainly their representatives spoke. However, Manmohan didn't stand in the way of listening to others who had additional grievances to air.

The similar type of exercise was repeated when we went to Ludhiana. By this time Manmohan had a full mental picture of the problems faced by these border towns and what kind of help was most feasible under the circumstances. These issues were carefully developed in the final report that was submitted.

When we met the Secretary of the Industry department in his office, Manmohan assured him that the report would be ready soon; and so it was.

That was Manmohan Singh who within this short period not only met the industrialists of the four important industrial destinations but also sorted out their specific problems as well as the strategy that needed to be adopted to stabilise industry in difficult pockets.

Manmohan was a teacher of par excellence. Even when allotted any area of Economics for classroom teaching—though his favourite was International Trade—he would see that lectures were delivered in simple easy-to-follow language and were logical. This approach was highly appreciated by students and little surprise that these were well attended. While in the department he would spend much of his time in his room preparing his lectures or attending to other activities where of course research found prime priority. He would not tolerate any teacher walking in his room aimlessly.

Of course, he was open to academic discussion with both teachers as well as students. He was happy to meet his colleagues over a cup of tea which also provided an opportunity to discuss current issues. In departmental meetings, he was forthright and would not even spare the Head of the

Department—Dr. S.B. Rangnekar who was also his teacher—if he found any of his decisions were arbitrary. Even he would not show any hesitation put down to resignation letter in case he found the behaviour of the VC or of the university was not in the overall interest of the university. He was a daring teacher.

It appears he had already developed links with the Central Government for during the summer vacation of 1965, I learnt from him that he was writing a report on behalf of Ministry of Foreign Trade which was then headed by Lalit Narain Mishra who was quite close to Mrs. Gandhi. In fact, after Manmohan returned from U.N.C.T.A.D. assignment he had joined this Ministry after a small stint with Delhi School of Economics.

Before joining the Central Government he had received offer from the U.N.C.T.A.D. (United Nations Conference on Trade and Development). Its Secretary-General Raul Prebisch, a famous Latin American economist, was looking for a young person who could help him in day-to-day business of this body as well as write policy papers and carry other related activities. It was a challenging job and it looks Mrs, Joan Robinson, who was also a teacher of Manmohan, had without any hesitation recommended Manmohan's name for this.

When offer was made to Manmohan he accepted it. But soon he learnt that knowledge of advanced statistic/ mathematics was also an essential qualification for this position, he immediately wrote that if it were so he was no longer interested in this job. Immediately came the reply that he should not have any such notion.

And his stint with the U.N.C.T.A.D. was so successful that when Raul Prebisch had visited Chandigarh, after the conclusion of the second conference of U.N.C.T.A.D. held in New Delhi, for receiving the degree of Honorary Doctorate from the Panjab University in a Special Convocation, he had told the Vice-Chancellor so. Even he had added that Manmohan was a gem that he was fortunate to have from this university. After the conclusion of the Convocation Manmohan had brought Raul Prebisch to the Department of Economics where both students and teachers were happy to meet this great economist in person.

After his stint with the U.N.C.T.A.D. and couple of years spent at the Delhi School of Economics, Manmohan had joined the Ministry of Foreign Trade as full time Economic Adviser. He had soon moved to the Ministry of Finance, first as its Economic Adviser, subsequently as full-fledged Secretary. While with the Ministry of Finance, Manmohan is said to have shown his expertise in preparing the Annual Budgets of the Government of India to the satisfaction of Mrs. Gandhi. Thus she had come to rely upon him.

After Finance, Manmohan moved to the Planning Commission. Here a special post of Member-Secretary had been created and Manmohan was the first to hold it. Next when there was a suitable opportunity in the Reserve Bank of India for its top post Manmohan was appointed as its Governor—another challenging position which Manmohan discharged with full confidence and honour.

From the RBI he was soon shifted back to the Planning Commission as its Deputy Chairman again the top job which was of the status of Cabinet Minister. It was done during the regime of Rajiv Gandhi.

I recollect V.K.R.V. Rao, another famous economist and also at one time Education Minister in the Cabinet of Indira Gandhi and also a great institution builder—for he created Delhi School of Economics, equally famous Institute of Economic Growth and the world renowned Institute of Social and Economic change (in Bangalore)—had once remarked that he had told Manmohan not to stick to a particular position for more than five years otherwise one would rot. And that one finds is true in the case of Manmohan's careergraph.

From Planning Commission he had moved to the South-South Commission as its Secretary-General with headquarters in Geneva. And after returning from there, with a small break he was appointed as Chairman in the University Grants Commission. The rest is all well known—his being highly successful Finance Minister (1991-96), after a break, the Leader of Opposition in the Rajya Sabha and now Prime Minister.

Manmohan Singh has been a rare careergrapher. I think there has been no other like instance. It is a rare honour for a person belonging to a humble family.

Book Published

Author of a book entitled "India's Export Trends and Prospects for Self-Sustained Growth", Clarendon Press, Oxford

University, 1964; also published a large number of articles in various economic journals.

Social and Cultural Activities, Literary, Artistic and Scientific Accomplishments and other Special Interests

Recipient of honorary degrees of D.Litt. from Panjab University, Chandigarh, Guru Nanak University, Amritsar, Delhi University, Delhi, Sri Venkateshwara University, Tirupathi, Punjabi University, Patiala, University of Mysore, Mysore, University of Bologna, Italy, Kurukshetra University, Kurukshetra, Osmania University, Hyderabad, Nagarjuna University, Nagarjunanagar and Dr. Bhimrao Ambedkar University, Agra; recipient of honorary degree of (i) Doctor of Laws from University of Alberta, Edmonton, Canada, (ii) Doctor of Social Sciences from University of Roorkee, Roorkee, (iii) D.Sc from Chaudhary Charan Singh Haryana Agricultural University, Hissar, (iv) Thapar Institute of Engineering and Technology, Patiala, (v) H.H. Kanchi Sri Parmacharya Award for Excellence, 1999, and (vi) Annasaheb Chirmule Award, 2000; Conferred, (i) University Medal for standing first in B.A. (Hons.), Economics, Panjab University, Chandigarh, 1952, (ii) Uttar Chand Kapur Medal, Panjab University, Chandigarh, for standing first in M.A. (Economics) 1954, (iii) Wright's Prize for distinguished performance at St. John's College, Cambridge, 1955 and 1957, (iv) Adam Smith Prize, University of Cambridge, U.K., 1956, (v) Padma Vibhushan, 1987, (vi) Euromoney Award, Finance Minister of the year, 1993, (vii) Asiamoney Award, Finance Minister of the year for Asia, 1993 and 1994, (viii) Jawaharlal Nehru Birth Centenary Award of the Indian Science Congress Association, 1994-95, (ix) Justice K.S. Hegde Foundation Award, 1996, (x) NIKKEI Asia Prize for Regional Growth by the Nihon Keizai Shimbun, Inc. (N.I.K.K.E.I.), publisher of Japan's leading business daily, 1997, and (xi) Lokmanya Tilak Award by the Tilak Smarak Trust, Pune, 1997.

Other Information

Elected, Wrenbury Scholar, University of Cambridge, 1957; Senior Lecturer in Economics, 1957-59; Reader in Economics, 1959-63; Professor, (i) Economics, Panjab University,

Chandigarh, 1963-65, and (ii) International Trade, Delhi School of Economics, University of Delhi 1969-71; Honorary Professor (i) Jawaharlal Nehru University, New Delhi, 1976, and (ii) Delhi School of Economics, University of Delhi, 1996; Economic Affairs Officer, 1966 and Chief, Financing for Trade Section, U.N.C.T.A.D., United Nations Secretariat, New York, 1966-69; Deputy for India in I.M.F. Committee of Twenty on International Monetary Reform, 1972-74; participated in Commonwealth Prime Ministers' Meeting, Kingston, 1975; Associate, Meetings of I.M.F. Interim Committee and Joint Fund-Bank Development Committee, 1976-80 and 1982-85; Fellow of the National Academy of Agricultural Science, New Delhi since 1999; National Fellow, National Institute of Education, N.C.E.R.T., 1986; Honorary Fellow, (i) St. John's College, Cambridge, U.K., 1982, (ii) Indian Institute of Bankers, 1982, (iii) All India Management Association, 1993, and (iv) Nuffield College, University of Oxford, Oxford, 1994; Leader, Indian Delegation to (i) Aid-India Consortium Meetings, 1977-79, (ii) Indo-Soviet Joint Planning Group Meeting, 1980-82, (iii) Indo-Soviet Monitoring Group Meeting, 1982, (iv) Commonwealth Heads of Government Meeting, Cyprus, 1993, and (v) Human Rights World Conference, Vienna, 1993; attended as member of Indian Delegations (i) Meeting of U.N.C.T.A.D. Trade and Development Board, Geneva, May 1971-July 1972, (ii) Ministerial Meeting of Group of 77, Lima, October 1971, (iii) Third Session of U.N.C.T.A.D., Santiago, April-May, 1972, (iv) Annual Meetings of I.M.F., I.B.R.D. and Commonwealth Finance Ministers, 1972-79, (v) Aid-India Consortium Meetings, Paris, 1973-79, (vi) Cancun Summit on North-South Issues, 1981, and (vii) South-South Consultations, New Delhi, 1982; represented Secretary-General, U.N.C.T.A.D. at several Inter-Governmental meetings, including Second Session of U.N.C.T.A.D, 1968 and Committee on Invisibles and Financing related to Trade Consultant to U.N.C.T.A.D., E.S.C.A.P. and Commonwealth Secretariat.

3

Leader of Economic Reforms : His Performance as a Finance Minister

Manmohan Singh's crystal clear views on the changing needs of the time are amply reflected in a lengthy interview that he gave to a representative of the press a few years back. While accepting the office of the Finance Minister (1991-96) he was quite certain that there was no other solution to India's slow economic growth and poor financial situation except embracing the path of globalisation and open market economy and also do away with license raj and bureaucratic hurdles. These controls though had served their purpose when the country was in their need but no longer. In fact, they were proving great hindrance in the country's growth. So earlier they were dismantled better it was.

In fact, his conviction for drastic change in the functioning of the Indian economy was strengthened when he saw the fast growing economies of east Asia and China. While they were just a few years earlier in no better situation than India, within this short-time of exposing them to the world trade, foreign investment and technology they had made rapid strides and left

India way behind. Particularly he was impressed by the Chinese amazing growth. Though a communist country she had seriously taken to the path of liberalisation which had resulted in several benefits.

And Manmohan was convinced that the time had come when India should also follow the path of these emerging economies if she wanted to become a world power.

Almost similar views have been highlighted in the following interview he had given to the press a few years ago. These are highly readable and convincing.

INDIA'S CENTRAL PLANNING : NEHRU'S VISION AND THE REALITY

Interviewer : Nehru wrote that socialism has science and logic on its side. What did he mean by that?

Manmohan Singh : Nehru was a rational thinker, and he wanted to apply science and technologies to solve the living problems of our time. In India, the foremost problem was India's economic [and] social backwardness [and] the great mass poverty that prevailed at the time of independence. Nehru's vision was to get rid of that chronic poverty, ignorance, and disease, making use of modern science and technology.

Interviewer : The central aim was to modernize, industrializing in one generation. Was that a crazy idea or a good idea?

Manmohan Singh : Elsewhere in the world, there are instances [of this happening]. The Soviet Union industrialized itself with a single generation. The industrial revolution in England you can break down into phases. A lot of structural changes took place in one generation, which later on became irreversible. That was Nehru's vision. His vision was to industrialize India, to urbanize India, and in the process he hoped that we would create a new society—more rational, more humane, less ridden by caste and religious sentiments. That was the grand vision that Nehru had.

Interviewer : In the end, did central planning get bogged down in itself? And what is your verdict on the concept of central planning, at least as a first phase?

Manmohan Singh : Let me say that I think the economic history of the last 150 years clearly shows that if you want to industrialize a country in a short period, let us say 20 years, and you don't have a well-developed private sector, entrepreneurial class, [then central planning is important].

Interviewer : What is your final verdict on central planning for India? Was it the right social [and economic plan]?

Manmohan Singh : In the initial stages of India's development central planning was a positive factor for development of promoting industrialization, of building industries which would never have [been] built. In terms of organizing science and technology, the new national laboratories came into being. If not for central planning, those things would never come into being.

But the real problem starts after 15 or 20 years, because the central planning system that we have evolved and [that] other countries have evolved lack an effective incentive system to modernize on a progressive basis, to improve productivity, to bring new technology. And that is where the failures of the central planning economy become far too big a burden to bear.

Interviewer : It's clear that the Soviet economy, with its Five-Year Plans, was an influence on India. Was the British Labor Party's mixed economy model also influential?

Manmohan Singh : Yes, I think India's economy always has been a mixed economy, and by Western standards we are much more of a market economy than a public sector-driven economy. The British idea of public sector and private sector coexisting greatly influenced Nehru's thinking. That was the modification that Nehru introduced over the Soviet planning model.

THE PERMIT RAJ AND ECONOMIC STAGNATION

Interviewer : Is it fair to say that the Permit Raj was almost an inevitable consequence of central planning?

Manmohan Singh : Yes, it was inevitable, because in an economy where resources are scarce [and] demands are too many, you need rationing, you need controls, and therefore you need permit license rights. In the initial stages, these controls were introduced in the name of introducing greater rationality into the allocation process. But after a period of time they became instruments of corruption. They became instruments of delay. They became instruments of uncertainty, and the economy simply could not get a clear sense of direction. Also, the information system that was necessary to rationally implement these controls, that also got bogged down, so I think it became a factor . . . .

Interviewer : Is it fair to say that to a certain extent the Permit Raj led to stagnation of the economy and the choking off of entrepreneurial growth?

Manmohan Singh : Yes, I think it gave rise to what I sometimes describe as functionalist capitalism. Capitalism historically has been a very dynamic force, and behind that force is technical progress, innovation, new ideas, new products, new technologies, and new methods of managing teams. If you have a rigidly controlled economy, cut-off from the rest of the world by infinite protection, nobody has any incentive to increase productivity and to bring new ideas. Therefore, the license Permit Raj became a great handicap in carrying forward the sustained process of sustained growth.

Interviewer : Is it fair to use the Ambassador car as an example of the lack of technical progress in a closed economy?

Manmohan Singh : Yes. I sometimes wonder [about that]. I think Toyota Motors and Nissan Motors came into existence at the same time. Nissan Motors got stuck with the Ambassador cars; Toyota became a world leader in the car industry. That's a measure of the lost opportunities as a consequence of being stuck at a very old-style model of license Permit Raj in a dominated economy.

Interviewer : Why did foreign trade play such a small part in India's economy for so long?

Manmohan Singh : In an economy of continental size, India is bound to be a relatively small proportion. Until very recently [in] the United States, I think trade [has been] only a small part of total national income. Even in Japan, for example, if you look at their exports, their exports are no more than 10 to 11 percent of their GDP. So it is very largely a consequence of the size of our economy. We are a country of continental dimension with large natural resources . . . . But in this case, [the tendency toward trade orientation] got further discouraged because of an inward-looking process of industrialization that we adopted.

THE WORLD OUTSIDE : THE INFLUENCE OF ASIAN GROWTH AND SOVIET COLLAPSE ON INDIA

Interviewer : You've already compared Toyota and Hindustan Motors. In the 1980s people started to look abroad. I think you yourself were struck by what was going in other parts of East Asia. Tell me what you were seeing and what you were thinking at that time, particularly with reference to South Korea.

Manmohan Singh : In the 1980s the Indian economy did reasonably well by world standards. Latin America and Africa were mired in their debt crisis. The Indian economy grew at 5.5 percent, but if you look at the last 30 years—for example, 1960 to 1985—the progress made by East Asian countries was phenomenal. In a single generation they had been able to transform the character of their economy. They were able to get rid of chronic poverty. Their achievements in terms of economic growth, in terms of social development are far more impressive than most other countries of the world. What happened in East Asia, particularly in a country like South Korea, did influence me very considerably.

Interviewer : Just taking South Korea as an example, am I right in saying that in about 1960 their living standards [and] the output of South Korea and India were the same?

Manmohan Singh : Yes, I think India and South Korea are roughly the same per capita income in 1960, and in 40 years time Korea has become a member of the OECD [Organization for Economic Cooperation and Development], and we are where we are.

Interviewer : And what's the difference in terms of per capita income?

Manmohan Singh : The Indian per capita income would be about $450. The Korean per capita income, if I remember correctly, about $11,000, $12,000 per annum.

Interviewer : All within one generation?

Manmohan Singh : Yes. That's a remarkable achievement.

Interviewer : Did this lead to the beginning of a change of heart in India when people looked at the other Asian economies?

Manmohan Singh : Certainly the fact that many countries of East Asia, much less well endowed than India, have marched far ahead of India's race for social and economic development has influenced a very considerable amount of thinking, particularly among economists and social scientists in the last decades.

Interviewer : What impact did the collapse [and] failure of the Soviet economic model have on people intellectually in India?

Manmohan Singh : This was telling proof that a command-type of economy was not as secure as we had thought. We thought [we] . . . could look at [the Soviet Union] as a new civilization. And here was an economy and its society and politics which could not defend itself against all the internal contradictions. Therefore, the collapse of the Soviet Union—the end of the Cold War was also a major factor—influenced thinking on economic reforms in our country, as it did other countries.

Interviewer : Did Mrs. Thatcher's attack on the mixed economy create waves over here?

Manmohan Singh : There are many people in India that admire Mrs. Thatcher. I've had the privilege of meeting her several times. I have great admiration for her, but I think she had a very limited influence on Indian thinking on economic reforms.

INDIA 1991 : "GETTING GOVERNMENT OFF THE BACKS OF THE PEOPLE"

Interviewer : Can you sum up the financial crisis in 1991? W was the situation India found herself in as you became finance minister?

Manmohan Singh : India had an unsustainable fiscal deficit. Our central government fiscal deficit was as high as 8.5 percent of GDP. India had an unsustainable balance-of-payments deficit. The current account deficit was close to 3.5 percent of GDP, and there were no foreign lenders who were willing to finance that deficit. Our foreign exchange reserves had literally disappeared, so we were on the verge of bankruptcy, and the nation faced an acute collapse of its economy.

Interviewer : How many days' worth of foreign currency [or reserves] did you have left?

Manmohan Singh : Our foreign-exchange reserves when I took over were no more than a billion dollars; that is, roughly equal to two weeks' imports.

Interviewer : So when you went to see the prime minister and brief him on the state of affairs, what did you say to him?

Manmohan Singh : I said to him that we are on the verge of a collapse. It is possible that we will still collapse, but there is a chance that if we take bold measures we may turn around, and that, I said, is an opportunity. We must convert this crisis into an opportunity to build a new India, to do things which many people before us have thought and said should be done, but somehow were never done.

Interviewer : And how did the prime minister react?

Manmohan Singh : The prime minister was very responsive. Without his active support and help, I could do nothing.

Interviewer : What about the rest of the party? There was quite a journey for them to make ideologically.

Manmohan Singh : We had not prepared the party for those major structural changes that we brought about within one month. But fortunately Rajiv Gandhi did a great service to our country, because he wrote the 1991 election manifesto of our party. In that election manifesto he had clearly recognized the need for economic reforms of the type which we undertook. It was an easy task for me to convince the skeptics in the party that I was not doing anything that was against the party. It is a legacy left to us by Rajiv Gandhi. That did not convince the critics, but that silenced them for quite some time.

Interviewer : When you stood up and made your famous speech in Parliament, what were the key arguments you used to persuade your colleagues to go along with you?

Manmohan Singh : The argument was quite simple. We were in the midst of an unprecedented crisis, and it was time to think big, not to shrink. We could, in a traditional way, tighten our belt, and we did that, tighten and tighten. But persistence on that path would have led to more misery, more unemployment, and I said there is an alternative path. Stabilization plus a credible structural adjustment program would shorten the period of misery. It would release the innovative spirit, [the] entrepreneurial spirits which were always there in India in [such] a manner that our economy would grow at a much faster pace, sooner than most people believed. That's exactly what happened.

Interviewer : In [that] speech you quoted Victor Hugo. Can you repeat that quote and tell us how you hoped it would apply to India?

Manmohan Singh : I quoted Victor Hugo's very famous sentence, "No power on earth can stop an idea whose time has come." I said to the Parliament, one month after I had taken over, that the emergence of India as a major global power, [an] economic power, is an idea whose time has come. I sincerely believe that if we did the things that I was saying to Parliament that they should do, no power on earth could stop the realization of this idea. So the dream was that we were in crisis, we should undertake basic structural changes. Out of that will emerge a new India, an India where there will be no poverty, the freedom from poverty, ignorance, and disease. You get that with India becoming a major global player in the world economy. That was the vision that inspired our economic reforms.

Interviewer : For a non-economist, non-Indian audience, what was the key change you made here?

Manmohan Singh : We got government off the backs of the people of India, particularly off the backs of India's entrepreneurs. We introduced more competition, both internal competition and external competition. We simplified and rationalized the tax system. We made risk-taking much more attractive . . . [and] much more profitable. So we tried to create an environment conducive to the growth of business.

Interviewer : And how about regulations and controls? What happened to those?

Manmohan Singh : We removed a large number of controls and regulations, which in the past had stifled the spirit of innovation, the spirit of entrepreneurship, and restricted the scope for competition, both internal competition and external competition. As a result, in the 1990s, productivity growth in the Indian industry has been much faster than ever before.

Interviewer : So that was the death of the Permit Raj?

Manmohan Singh : Well, I hope that was the death. We still need to do a lot more things to remove the [effects] of the license Permit Raj.

Interviewer : When do you think India could reach a level of real prosperity?

Manmohan Singh : We were there [in power] only for five years. Out of these five years, two to three years were very turbulent years. We have masked the monetary controversies. We were not in power for the last four years, and the political developments in India, although the direction of economic policy remains essentially what we laid out, the pace has not been to our liking. I think the pace has slowed down, and that certainly worries me. If we had gotten another five years I think we would have ensured that by the year 2010 or 2015 many of the dreams we had [would have] become a reality.

Interviewer : You've said how you see the future for India. But in that future, what would the role of government be?

Manmohan Singh : The role of government is not a government that will disappear. They share our public expenditure. Total national expenditure of India is only about 30 percent. It's much lower than the United States, much lower than the United Kingdom and many European countries. We are not saying that government will disappear. We're going to redirect this expenditure. The government will take a lot more interest in education, in primary health care, in environmental protections, in promoting research and development. But the government will not be in the business of running industries and running trading enterprises.

It is restructuring the role of the government, getting government out of activities where governments are not very efficient at doing things, getting government more actively involved where we feel markets alone cannot provide the necessary amount of goods to the extent that our people need—basic education, basic health care, environmental protection measures, basic social safety net. These are the things that we feel our country needs, and in a civilized society governments have a major responsibility to provide these basic public goods.

Interviewer : Is India's very successful information technology industry a product of liberalization?

Manmohan Singh : In a way it's a product of both the level of development that India has had in the last 50 years and the great centers of science and technology. We also have a very sizeable industrial base. So I think that [the] contribution of history has to be acknowledged.

At the same time, if the information technology industry had been regulated in the same way as we had regulated other industries, I think that revolution also would have been stopped in its infancy.

One good fortune is [that] the information technology sector has been left alone. Government has played a more promotional role, but not a regulatory role, and that's why I think the favoring of creativity, the favoring of entrepreneurship . . . was a help.

EMBRACING GLOBALIZATION AND UNDERSTANDING THE RISKS

Interviewer : You're quoted as saying "self-reliance means trade, not aid." You said earlier that India was more of a big continental economy that didn't need to trade too much. What do you mean?

Manmohan Singh : What I was saying when we talked of self-reliance means that India has to be integrated into the evolving world economy. We have to share in the benefits of an increasingly interdependent economy. Trade offers opportunities; it creates an environment in which our industry can grow at a rate faster than domestic demand.

The opening of capital markets offers opportunities for us to increase our investment beyond the rate of domestic savings. India should take full advantage of these opportunities of an increasingly globalized economy.

At the same time there are risks, because competition is a two-edged weapon. It helps those who are strong; it hurts those who are weak. India must strengthen its capabilities to withstand the onslaught of competition. The [competitive] process creates an environment in which India's enormous latent strengths in terms of entrepreneurship [and] creative ability could make India one of the global players.

So self-reliance as I saw it meant not making India dependent on foreigners for savings, though we opened up India to increase participation by foreign capital. But I never believed that foreigners could underwrite the development of India. That task will have to be done within India. But [it should be done] in a manner in which the bulk of savings for India's development would continue to be generated domestically.

Interviewer : So you see globalization in the main as a net gain for India?

Manmohan Singh : It offers opportunities, but problem areas . . . . For example, we are part of the world trading system. There are opportunities, but also the introduction of a large number of extraneous elements into Uruguay [the 1986-94 Uruguay Round]. For example, the TRIPs [the International Property Council of the WTO] legislation has created burdens in terms of the prices of essential drugs. The TRIPs legislation is a negative.

The opening up of agriculture [is another] example. Our agriculture is not subsidized. Agriculture in Europe and America is highly subsidized. Now, if you're going to have a world situation in which the highly subsidized agricultures of Europe and America are going to compete against the non-subsidized agriculture of India, I worry about that. But I do believe they're taking pluses and minuses. India has every reason to be a part of the world trading system.

Interviewer : Some people would say that the rules aren't fair, that the powerful countries, the rich countries set the rules, and it'll always be to the disadvantage of the emerging countries like yours.

Manmohan Singh : That's certainly true. The international economic game is a power game, and those who are strong are always able to lay down the laws of the game. As I see it, India is not strong enough to rewrite the rules of the world game in its own image. But there are opportunities, and [other] countries of East Asia have taken advantage of those opportunities of the trading system, which has many minus points, also.

India has to do the same thing, taking advantage of these opportunities to realize its destiny, and in the process hope that in due course of time we will be strong enough to also influence the writing of the rewriting of the rules of the game.

Interviewer : Do you think that globalization will help to solve India's perennial problems of poverty?

Manmohan Singh : Globalization creates opportunities. As I said, freer trade, if it is genuinely free, and India's labor-intensive products can find markets abroad that will help to get new jobs in our country. That will help to relieve poverty.

In the same way, if we have access to first-class technology, then we don't have to reinvent the wheel. We can cut short the process of modernizing our economy. In the same way, opening up of the capital markets [and] freer flow of capital can increase our rate of investment [and] the rate of growth at a rate faster than the rate of domestic savings.

But as I said before, our competition is a two-way street. If we do not educate our people, then there is great danger that in the type of world economy that is now on the horizon, the knowledge-centered world economy, it is only the skilled workers who are going to be the biggest beneficiary of the growth processes. If India's working force is not adequately educated, then globalization will lead to the destruction of many of our traditional industries.

It is our responsibility to ensure that globalization becomes a positive game, and of course we need the rest of the world as help to see that the international economic environment remains supportive of the needs of the poorer countries.

THE POWER OF PROTEST : FORCING CHANGE OR PERPETUATING MISERY?

Interviewer : Globalization and change generally brings disruption. Take blue-collar workers in America, or farmers in America. The competition from countries like India is going to cost jobs and livelihoods, their whole way of life. Do you see the pendulum swinging back, abroad or here, against globalization?

Manmohan Singh : In this country there are worries. I mentioned the intellectual property rights, classes of the WTO agreement, [and] the opening up of agricultural markets. We are going this year to remove all quantitative import restrictions, and there are worries in several segments of our industry that this is going to hurt our industry. But I do believe that we have enough instruments in our system to ensure that the damage can be contained.

Interviewer : What's your reaction to the anti-capitalist, anti-WTO campaign, and its legitimacy?

Manmohan Singh : Let me say that there are people in the West who would like to further go on the road to rewrite the rules of the game. The needs of U.S. labour, for example, all this talk of introducing labour standards into WTO negotiations, environmental standards.

These are non-trade issues. The American attempt at Seattle to introduce these extraneous issues really created serious doubts in the minds of many developing countries that new protectionism was back in the West in the guise of labour standards, social standards, and environment. I sincerely believe that the West should resist using the WTO as an instrument to promote these causes.

This is not to say that labour standards are not important, our environmental standards are not important, but we have international institutions. The ILO [International Labour Organization] is there; the UNIP [United National Independence Party] is there. Those things should be dealt with in those [organizations]. But to do these things as sanctions in trading relations will perpetuate the inequities of the present trading system, where the stronger countries always dictate the rules of the game.

Interviewer : One of the cases that often comes up if you talk to anti-WTO people is child labour. You know Britain abolished child labour in about 1814, the United States in about 1930, 1935. How would you argue that from your point of view?

Manmohan Singh : We are not saying that we have a right to employ child labour. Our national legislation does recognize that this is a curse. All of our children should be in schools. But by using the practice of child labour as an excuse to impose restrictions on India's labour-intensive products, is it going to help those children? It's just going to perpetuate the misery. It is going to reduce our country's ability to find resources to deal with the causes of those children not being in school.

Interviewer : What about the legitimacy of the anti-WTO demonstrators? Who do they represent?

Manmohan Singh : I think this is a strange coalition, quite frankly. I do not want to question [their] motives. Many of them are highly motivated, international-spirited, but it appears to me that the extreme right or the extreme left have got to come together, just as sometimes I feel that [they must] when it comes to population control. Both the extreme right and the extreme left seem to agree, and this is another instance where the two seem to have coalesced.

SINGH THE ECONOMIST : TRAINED IN ONE SCHOOL OF THOUGHT, SUBSCRIBING TO ANOTHER

Interviewer : You were rather surprised when you were invited to be finance minister. But how did it actually happen?

Manmohan Singh : You should ask that question from Prime Minister Rao. I was very surprised when this news was conveyed to me. I didn't believe it. When I asked some friends of mine they said, "You're going to become the scapegoat. You're going to fail and maybe within six months you will be out." And I said I was the Fagin of my peers. I'd held all the top civil service jobs, but here was an opportunity to play a political role, and there was an odd chance that we would make a success of it, in which case I would have a footnote in India's history. If I fail, that's of no great consequence. And who fails if India wins?

Interviewer : Did you have any trepidation when you stepped into this role?

Manmohan Singh : I had trepidation, but somehow I was convinced that we would go through. I said to the country on the day I became finance minister that the economy was in such bad shape that you shouldn't expect any major rewards for the next three years. All I can promise is blood, sweat, and tears. But quite frankly I think that the economy turned around much sooner, much quicker, and much more deeply than I had anticipated. That's why our critics were completely silenced. They were predicting massive doses of unemployment.

Nothing of that sort happened. Indian industry boomed. All segments of Indian industry—capital goods, consumer goods, intermediate products—grew. We created a record number of jobs. We were able to control inflation and the economy was growing at the rate of 7 percent per annum.

Interviewer : You studied economics at Cambridge and Oxford. What was the prevailing orthodoxy when you were a student? What did you embody?

Manmohan Singh : I had the privilege of being taught by stalwarts like Joan Robinson, Nicholas Kaldor, Richard Kahn, Maurice Dobb, and Sir Dennis Robertson. I think the predominant mood of the times at that time was that you need strong government intervention, along the Keynesian theme, to stabilize the capitalist economy; that in poor countries you need strong government intervention to move the economy onto a path of self-sustained growth.

Interviewer : If they saw you now they'd be spinning in their graves, wouldn't they?

Manmohan Singh : At that time whosoever came to India, whether they came from MIT or from Cambridge, England, the advice to the country was almost the same. If you really want to take off into self-sustained growth, to use the famous phrase, the government has to be the major leading player.

4

Transformation Agenda : Manmohan Singh's First Address to the Nation as a Prime Minister

It is unfortunate after the President's Address to the joint session of both the houses of Parliament, the government was not allowed to function. There were continuous disturbances in both the Houses by the Opposition Parties on the issue of induction of tainted members into the ministry. The Opposition Parties demanded that unless they were removed such disturbances would continue.

Under the circumstances Manmohan Singh was not able to function, nor even deliver his first speech in the Parliament.

To get over this hindrance he chose to speak straight to the Nation on the electronic media.

As one goes through the Address one notices that while it is a close elaboration of the common man's transformation agenda agreed upon to be followed by the present government, the way it has been drafted, the simplicity and clarity of the language used and Manmohan's forthright views on how the government would function to achieve the programme—speak high of his scholarship and vision.

It is reproduced on the next page :

"My Fellow Citizens,

"I speak to you with a deep sense of humility, fully conscious of the sacred responsibility entrusted to me. You have assigned the task of governance of our country to the United Progressive Alliance and its supporting parties. You have delivered your verdict and the verdict is clear. You have sought a change in the manner in which this country is run, a change in national priorities, and a change in the processes and focus of governance. You have, through your mandate, made it clear that economic growth has to be accompanied by equity and social justice. You have expressed concern for the poor and disadvantaged sections of our society and for minorities and backward regions to be at the heart of all policies of the government.

"As I share with you the priorities of our government, I am reminded of the Father of our Nation, Mahatma Gandhi. Gandhiji had said that his mission in life was "to wipe every tear from every eye." Think of the poorest person you have ever seen, Gandhiji would say, "and ask if your next act will be of any use to him." That message of Bapu resonates in our ears as we settle down to the business of government.

"The National Common Minimum Programme has been prepared by us keeping in mind the priorities brought into focus by your mandate. The Address of the President of India to Parliament outlines a comprehensive agenda for the nation to which our government is committed. The country would have benefited if Parliament had been allowed to discuss the President's Address. I was eagerly looking forward to contributions from all parties in this discussion. Unfortunately, this was not allowed to happen. It should be a matter of deep concern for all of us when established mechanisms for a constructive dialogue and critique, which are vital for a parliamentary democracy, are disrupted and not allowed to operate.

"Parliament is a forum which is sacred and it must be our collective endeavour to ensure that we maximize its effectiveness. I request parties across the entire political spectrum to respect Parliament as an essential forum for public debate so that we can move forward on the task of nation-building which is a common goal for one and all.

"We can justly take pride in the fact that since Independence we have been able, with our efforts, to build the foundations of a modern economy and record an acceleration in the rate of economic growth. There have been impressive gains in terms of the educational and health status of the nation. However, the benefits of this performance have not touched all our citizens in equal measure. Growth is not an end in itself. It is a means to generate employment, banish poverty, hunger and homelessness and improve the standard of living of the mass of our people. It must also be environmentally sustainable.

"Equity and efficiency are complimentary, not contradictory, and we must move forward on both these while maintaining a high degree of fiscal and financial discipline, and a robust external economic profile.

"To be able to devote our attention and energy to economic development that improves the lives of our people, we must ensure social and political stability, communal harmony and respect for the rule of law. We must put in place policies and programmes which empower all our citizens to lead a life of dignity and self-respect. Our government is committed to the security and welfare of all minorities, the protection of the interests of the scheduled castes and scheduled tribes, of backward classes and all weaker sections. Equally we are committed to the empowerment of women. We will ensure equal participation of all in the processes of governance.

"The essence of the National Common Minimum Programme is the recognition that policies that are aimed at promoting economic growth must also advance the cause of distributive justice and create new employment opportunities. Economic reform is not only about freeing private enterprise from the shackles of bureaucratic control. It is also about making the government more effective, efficient and people friendly so that it can handle better the many tasks that only Governments can perform. And, it is also about ensuring fair and transparent regulation of the market where this is necessary. While many in our country are benefiting from their integration into the market and the global economy, millions of our citizens are still plagued by illiteracy, disease, want, hunger and malnutrition. Gender disparities are high and educational, nutritional and health levels of women are much lower than of men. Chronic poverty afflicts millions who lack income and food security. This is particularly acute among the scheduled castes, other backward castes and scheduled tribes. At a regional level, too, the disparities are high and while some regions of the country seem to be on an accelerating growth path, there is a concern that other regions are not only lagging but are also falling behind. Regretably, minorities suffer from not only economic insecurity but also a sense of marginalization from political and governance processes.

"As a nation, we cannot accept such disparities. We have been given a mandate which enjoins us to be sensitive to the concerns of these deprived sections and regions. We have an obligation to ensure that they too benefit from growth in full measure. Our commitment to investments in the social sectors is rooted in this reality. It is the responsibility of government, at all levels, at the Centre, in the States and at the level of the community, to address each of these economic and social challenges. However, I am convinced that the government, at every level, is today not adequately equipped and attuned to deal with this challenge and meet the aspirations of the people. To be able to do so, we require the reform of government and of public institutions. Much of the focus of economic reforms in the past decade has been on reducing the role of the government in controlling the Private Sector; controls that hampered entrepreneurial dynamism and often bred corruption. This was necessary. Yet, there are many areas, critical areas, that directly affect the quality of life of every citizen, where the government has a role, and is expected by every citizen to have a role. These include the provision of social and physical infrastructure for development, the provision of elementary education and public health, providing drinking water and sanitation. They also include economic infrastructure which in our country in large part must be provided by the Government such as irrigation, power, roads and railways. Our people expect the government to be pro-active and sensitive to their needs. In each of these areas, at every level of governance, the reform of government is today an urgent task before us.

"We will pursue economic reform and widen the space for individual initiative and enterprise, but even as we do so, we cannot forsake the obligation of running a government that works, and works for the people. The reform of administration and of public institutions to improve efficiency and the quality of delivery services will be our immediate priority.

"There has been a neglect of the interests of the farmers in recent years and this is reflected in a significant slowing down in agricultural growth in the past five years. Farmers in many parts of the country have faced distress and there has been no helping hand. The National Common Minimum Programme of the United Progressive Alliance is committed to giving a "New Deal" to rural India. Agriculture must receive the priority attention it deserves. Public and private investment in agriculture has to be greatly increased. A key concern in recent years has been the lack of access to credit. Our government is already addressing this issue directly by pursuing policies that improve the farmer's access to affordable credit. Agricultural research, training and extension also require much greater attention. I would like to see the emergence of new centers of excellence in agriculture as we have in technology and management. There has to be a sharper focus on expanding opportunities for gainful employment in agriculture and in off-farm rural activities. Food for Work Programme, efficiently implemented, can greatly assist in achieving this objective.

"The Indian farmer has also suffered from too many controls and restrictions. There are still far too many internal barriers to trade that must go. We must also re-examine those aspects of our policies that prevent a creative interaction between farmers and agro-industries. I would like to see the creation of a "Single Market" across the country for both manufactured and agricultural produce with encouragement of agro-industry linkages. With the introduction of value-added taxation this integration of the Indian market will be further enabled.

"A striking feature of development in our country has been the rapid increase in urbanization. There are now more than 30 cities with a population of more than one million. The rapid and unplanned growth of these cities has contributed to increased urban pollution, crime and absence of the required infrastructure like access to drinking water, sanitation, roads, footpaths for pedestrians and public spaces, parks and greenery is making life in urban India a living hell for many. Most of the responsibility for this rests with States and Municipal Governments. It will be our effort to give special attention to policies that can encourage urban development and urban renewal. We will actively seek public-private partnership in building urban infrastructure in a planned manner.

"Higher rates of economic growth, urbanization and the modernization of agriculture will continue to increase the demand for energy. This demand can only be met with new investment, increased efficiency and rational pricing. Even as we plan to make more efficient use of conventional sources of energy, we must invest in the development of non-conventional sources. We will evolve an Energy Policy package that will cover all sources of energy and will address all aspects like energy security, access and availability, affordability and pricing, efficiency and environment.

"Water has emerged as a critical and contentious issue across the country. Even access to safe drinking water remains a problem in many parts of our country. Water management policies have to be so formulated as to address the needs of farmers and weaker sections, especially women, as well as those of city-dwellers. We will have to find innovative, cost-effective and community-based solutions. Groundwater replenishment and management and rainwater harvesting require close cooperation between government, panchayati raj institutions and non-governmental organizations. The government will reverse the neglect of public investment in irrigation, addressing the specific problems of each river basin, in an environment and people friendly manner.

"We need new thinking in health policy. While the government will continue to help in the growth of private and community-based health and medical care, there is a crying need for the reform of public health and public hospitals. We will make public hospitals more efficient and accessible, through public-private partnership aimed at offering affordable and humane health care. We need community-based and public health oriented solutions to tackling communicable diseases, epidemics, especially HIV/AIDS, and disability management and population stabilisation.

"People are a nation's greatest resource. Our greatest asset will be an educated and capable work force. Our government will work along with State governments to step up public spending on education, to universalize access to elementary education and to improve the quality of our education. We shall make effective use of mid-day meals programme for school children to achieve this objective. I am particularly concerned about the access to schooling and higher education of children belonging to scheduled castes and scheduled tribes, weaker sections and minorities.

"The education of the girl child and female literacy will be priority areas for us. We will do our utmost to provide scholarships to help them acquire the training and skills that can make them self-reliant and proud citizens. Our children need modern and relevant education aimed at making them concerned, capable and caring citizens of the Republic.

"Our economy has been rapidly integrating with the global economy over the past decade, with a growing sense of self-confidence. However, domestic enterprise needs world class and cost-effective infrastructure. Better roads, better connectivity, modern airports and railways, efficient ports and affordable and reliable power are all the basic requirements for a competitive economy. For centuries India has been a trading nation, actively engaged in the movement of goods and people across continents and high seas. We will pursue policies that enable our economy to be better integrated with the world economy without hurting the interests of our people. We will create an environment conducive to the utilization of the talent pool of the vast and diverse Indian diaspora. We greatly value their participation in the development of our nation.

"No objective in this development agenda can be met if we do not reform the instrument in our hand with which we have to work, namely, the government and public institutions. Clearly, this will be my main concern and challenge in the days to come.

"We will maintain our tradition of an independent foreign policy, built on a national consensus and based on our supreme national interests. We will expand our network of international relationships—preserving solidarity with traditional allies and strengthening new partnerships. We will work with like-minded nations for an equitable, multi-polar world order, which takes into account the legitimate aspirations of developing countries.

"We desire to live in a neighbourhood of peace and prosperity. We will actively pursue the composite dialogue with Pakistan. We are sincere about discussing and resolving all issues, including Jammu & Kashmir. We recognize that resolution of major issues requires national consensus and accommodation of public sentiment in both countries. It is self-evident that terrorism and violence would cast a dark shadow over this process. With our other South Asian neighbours, it will be our sincere effort to jointly realize the vast potential for cooperation, and to ensure mutual security, stability and development.

"In our relations with China, we are encouraged by positive developments, which we are committed to strengthening. Bilateral economic cooperation has shown remarkable growth and diversification. We shall carry forward the process of discussion to resolve the boundary question from the political perspective of our bilateral relations.

"As two of the world's great democracies, our strengthened relationship with USA is a fact of considerable importance. The transformation of our relations with USA has been supported by the expansion of economic links and people to people ties, including the presence of almost a million people of Indian origin in that country. We will welcome the expansion of cooperation between the two Governments to include new and mutually beneficial areas, particularly high technology.

"The strength and vibrancy of our partnership with Russia has withstood the flux of the post-Cold War world. We will accelerate the diversification of our relationship, particularly in defence, high technology, space and nuclear energy, while intensifying economic cooperation.

"We have traditionally strong relations with the countries of South-east and West Asia, based on cultural affinities, economic interaction and a vibrant Indian expatriate community. We aim to build upon these. While speaking of West Asia, I must share our deep concern about developments in Iraq and the suffering of the people of that country. It is our earnest hope that democracy would be restored and full sovereignty transferred to a truly representative Government of Iraq. India is committed to participate in all endeavours aimed at bringing stability and to ensure the well-being of the Iraqi people.

"We will also strengthen our bilateral relations with developing countries of Latin America and Africa. Similarly, strong ties with the nations of Central Asia are of importance for our international trade, as well as for our strategic and energy security.

"We will actively pursue a cooperative relationship with the European Union to expand the political and economic frontiers of collaboration. We welcome the inclusion of many new member-states, with whom we have a long tradition of cooperation.

"I wish to place on record the nation's deep sense of gratitude and pride in the gallantry, valour, professionalism and the spirit of self-sacrifice of our armed forces. I assure the nation that we will not be found wanting in providing for our armed forces, or in caring for our ex-servicemen. We will streamline defence acquisition procedures, so that our forces obtain modern weapon systems and technologies. Our government will ensure that the necessary funds are made available for these purposes.

"We will maintain a credible minimum nuclear deterrent, along with a policy of 'no first use' in our nuclear doctrine. India is a responsible nuclear power, and we will continue to work to prevent proliferation of weapons of mass destruction. At the same time, we remain committed to the goal of universal nuclear disarmament.

"Internal security remains an important challenge. Terrorism poses a grave threat to the unity and progress of our nation. We shall combat it with all the resources at our command. There shall be no doubt whatsoever about our resolve to deal with this insidious threat to our nation.

"The government will continue the process of dialogue with the Hurriyat and all other groups in Jammu and Kashmir. The Government is willing to talk with all disaffected groups provided they shun the path of violence.

"We will adopt a comprehensive approach to the problem of national security, to create greater synergy between our intelligence agencies, closer coordination between internal security structures, more efficient civil-military interface and more effective harnessing of technology to national security management.

"My fellow citizens, I share the feeling of well-meaning citizens when they express pained concern about the decline of morals and ethics in public life. There is, however, no better way to deal with this incipient threat to our democracy than to meet it head on by joining public life ourselves.

"When I chose to enter public life I did so because I was convinced that our democracy needs more professionals to become more engaged and active in politics.

"I, therefore, now appeal to each one of you to also participate in our public life so that governments at all levels—central, state and local—are all constantly put on notice and not just tested once in five years.

"When I travel across the country I am always heartened by the increasing number of young and idealistic people I meet who work with voluntary organizations, empowering the dispossessed and the dis-enfranchised. We shall make effective use of the resources of the civil society to improve the quality of governance and delivery of important public services.

"Fellow citizens, I urge you to come forward and take an active role in the nation's public affairs. Each one of you can make a difference. I seek your support to restore to our public life a greater sense of purpose and a renewed commitment to decency, morality and the hard work needed to take our country and every one of our citizens forward. We must re-capture the spirit of idealism and self-sacrifice which characterized the high noon of our freedom struggle. Working together, we shall ensure that this ancient sacred land of ours regains its rightful place in the comity of nations."

5

Commonman Emerges as a Hero : UPA's First National Budget

The national budget is the most important document for it tells the state of fiscal health of the country. It is only a strong budget with liberal foreign exchange position, prosperous trade, growing revenue, declining fiscal deficit and other positive aspects that would indicate its rising prosperity. A weak budget on the other hand would show just the opposite.

This chapter is divided into three sections. Section 1 is based on an exercise by the author on the 1994-95 budget—what it should be like? During that time to suggest a commonman's budget with emphasis on poverty eradication programmes, which exactly I did in this budget, would have been just laughed at, when the Congress government was pursuing with full vigour the policies of globalisation and liberalisation which though brought prosperity in urban areas, failed to touch the rural areas with the result that level of growth in these two areas continued to widen apart.

And today it is exactly the highlighting of this skewed growth between rural and urban areas that has become the main pillar of Congress-led government's agenda.

Thus, while the neglect of rural areas and rising poverty

and unemployment in the 1996 elections led to the downfall of the Congress government, almost eight years later it was the same neglect that had led to the downfall of BJP-led government and victory for the Congress for projecting rural poverty and unemployment.

In Section 2 we have presented the text of the national budget presented recently in the Parliament by the finance minister P. Chidambaram, and in Section 3 it is the critique's view about the budget. The main criticism is the omission of any concrete policy/programme for the early job creation.

Section 1

Here is reproduced my dream budget of 1994-95 ("Manmohan's India", pp. 101-06).

"EXERCISE IN 1994-95 BUDGET— WHAT IT SHOULD BE LIKE?

"Here an attempt is made on the budget exercise for the year 1994-95. Should it follow the earlier approach of the present government? Or should it have a different approach? If different, on what lines it should be different? And so on.

"At the outset it be said that budgets so far presented, as also observed earlier, have faithfully followed the approach ot globalising the Indian economy through structural reforms, privatisation and market economy. Naturally with this background budgets have had liberal approach towards the growth of private sector, particularly encouraging investment by the multinational firms and clearing all possible road blocks in their way. The recent (1993-94) budget has provided maximum possible concession to the growth of private sector industry where large industry in particular has been favoured. As well concessions offered to consumer industries, though stated to benefit consumers, actually have amounted to encouraging large-scale consumer industries where the multinational firms have been especially encouraged to play a leading role.

"Also the freeing of foreign trade sector of cumbersome rules and regulations, is again mainly for the benefit of foreign multinational firms so that they have liberal access to the Indian market, rather than help the overall growth process of the domestic economy. As a matter of fact how such approach has resulted in throwing the doors of this country open the dumping tactics of foreign firms in the West as well Japan, has already become quite obvious in the nature of recent imports which are having an adverse impact on the growth of domestic industries. Thus, if proper measures are not adopted to counter such nasty dumping tactics of foreign firms, where the government has already lacked courage, India would soon become heaven for foreign goods.

"Similarly when we talk of encouraging exports through providing all possible assistance, we forget that with over four decades of the functioning with highly protected domestic market, one could not expect much change at least in a short period in our export trade. What little experience there is it shows that, despite setting up of 100 per cent export units where the shrewd and manipulating manufacturers have amassed several hundred crores by befooling both the government as well the public, does not make encouraging reading. Most of these units have been set-up basically with an idea to get liberal concessions and subsidies from the government as well raise equally liberal resources from the Indian public by painting a highly promising picture. Excepting a few units, others have yet to establish their credibility.

"Further in our craze for high-tech growth and for complete modernisation of the economy, we have unfortunately forgotten the common man, his basic needs, his employment problem and how hard he has been affected with the present policies. In fact, over-involvement with the advanced countries' model of structural reforms, does not leave time with our politicians and bureaucrats to look into the issues that confront the common man. In fact, the budgets have been completely silent in this respect.

"Thus it would be very appropriate if we were to look into the problems and needs of the common man more carefully in our next budget. In fact the next budget should be common man's budget where policies framed and resource allocation made take into consideration the total needs of ordinary citizens.

"When we talk of common man, it is quite obvious that in

our society it is only a small percentage of population—between five to 10—who are likely to benefit from the present structural reform policies, while these policies ignore an overwhelming majority of the population.

"Just come to think of high consumerism that has captured the urban society in a big way. But then, how many people even among the urban society are in a position to benefit from such consumerism? Further by exposing each and everyone of them to all that goes under high consumer society, we are trying allure them to become a part of such society without providing most of them even with means to satisfy their basic needs. This has its adverse impact and encourages lawlessness, terrorism, insecurity of life, and several other negative impacts. Already we have witnessed them in different parts of the country.

"In fact with the rise of gun power and terrorism, the cost of security too has risen substantially. Thus, what purpose is served to have these reforms which only add up to more unemployment, gun power and security cost?

"The roots of such adverse development are naturally to be found in our quick advance towards high western styled consumer society, where foreign multinational firms have played significant role. It is time we had a realistic approach and turned our attention more to the production of those goods that satisfy the basic needs of the population. Unfortunately with our openness and privatisation approach we have not paid adequate attention to the basic needs of consumers—here particularly the foodgrains have been getting highly expensive during the last couple of years. It has witnessed price rise which was not to be witnessed over the last couple of decades.

"In fact if we want to serve the interest of common man, who, as it is well-known, has to live on his petty income—may be from a small, unproductive farm or on a low income service or as a daily wage worker—the only way to help him is to provide him the basic necessities of life at a price he can afford. Now with the existing inflated prices of wheat and rice, it certainly becomes difficult for him to buy sufficient quantity of foodgrains. May be, under these circumstances, we have to restore subsidies which earlier had played an important role in keeping down the food prices.

"We will also have to streamline the public distribution

system if it has to serve the needs of common man. Here again foodgrains and other essential items should be available at prices which ordinary citizens can afford. So both subsidies and public distribution system should find an important place in the budget.

"As well employment problem, which is the most crucial problem facing the country, should get special attention. The recent budgets have been completely silent on this issue. In fact it appears it was thought that through the growth of private sector after reforms, the employment problem would be automatically solved.

"But under the Indian setting this is not going to happen. As a matter of fact here we need a different type of approach to both industries as well services for generating the maximum possible employment opportunities. It is well-known that large industries, using the latest technology and mostly highly capital-intensive, do not have large employment avenue. At the same time because of the nature of technology these are looking for mostly skilled manpower and there is little demand for unskilled labour. Thus, under such framework which is getting further strengthened with current structural reforms, India's unskilled millions who enter the labour market annually do not have much scope for relief.

"They could be best accommodated in small/medium industries as well in simple services, and for these there exists substantial scope. Thus, our attention should now be concentrated on more and more small and medium industries than on large, highly sophisticated industries which in fact cut down on employment.

"It is interesting to find that only a handful of multinational firms have the control over modern consumer industries. They deploy all possible means to control the largest possible share of the market. So far instead of disciplining their hegemony, we have only let them grow stronger and now under the present approach of the government, it would be quite difficult to penetrate into their areas.

"This shows how our policies have encouraged concentration of production, instead of its diversification for helping different regions as well employed.

"The budget therefore needs to make some positive

approach in the direction of encouraging production of those consumer goods which are currently controlled by a handful of such manufactures so that the benefit could flow to a larger segment of the domestic manufacturers.

"The budget should also adopt positive policy towards public sector undertakings. The past couple of years experience has shows that quite a few loss sustaining units have now turned the corner and are on the way of encouraging performance. As a matter of fact the government itself has by and large been responsible for the poor performance of these units, with its over-socialistic bias under which it had loaded it with surplus manpower which adds to a hefty wage bill as well as had adopted unproductive price policies in the name of social welfare. If both these issues are carefully sorted out there is no reason why the public sector units should not be able to compete with private units. Already we have seen that the sale of government share in the public sector units has not brought any tangible benefit either to the government or to the country. As well the 'golden hand shake' policy adopted in case of workers thrown out from the loss sustaining units, has not worked to the interest of affected workers.

"Briefly the next budget should devote its attention to ameliorate the lot of common man who infact has been the worst affected during the past couple of years. If subsidies on food inputs cannot be restored then at least it should be laid down that all the money thus collected would be exclusively utilised for the improvement of rural infrastructure, particularly in those places which are still inaccessible and are by and large inhabited by the poor people like the scheduled castes and tribals. Similarly, poor consumers affected by the price hike in foodgrains should be adequately compensated by the availability of highly subsidised food, articles from the public distribution system, especially earmarked to serve the needs of these people. For this the budget should make adequate provision. The budget as a long-term strategy should help the poor in strengthening their food security by creating individual household storage facility at a time when food prices are generally low.

"The budget should also have a positive approach to strengthen the medium and small industries and provide possible facilities, including liberal funs for encouraging their growth on healthy lines. At the same time there is need to have a second thought on the budget allocation to the current rural development bodies, like Khadi and Village Industries Commission, which have outlived their utility and where much of their budget is incurred in bureaucrats and other urban employees as well on rental and maintaining a chain of emporia in the posh urban areas, rather than for the benefit of rural people. With some thought this budget could be more productively utilised on sustainable and high growth rural industries like agro-industries.

"The budget should also provide more funds of the basic services like medical, education, urban transport and power as well research particularly in areas which can bring about quick transformation of the rural economy where, besides agriculture, there is good scope for starting several modern industries.

"As well there is special need for providing funds for the transformation of tribal societies. Here, for instance, in the North-East and even elsewhere still there persists the practice of shifting agriculture, that is the system clearing of a particular patch of jungle-land through burning for agriculture. In this way a large portion of forest area is lost every year. Further as this practice has been going on for a number of years and also there has been high population pressure, a major chunk of forest land in this country has already been lost and created ecological problem. It is therefore essential that special funds under the budget are allocated to the tribal areas for discouraging this practice and instead encouraging settled land-use as well providing alternative job opportunities to the affected population."

Section 2

TEXT OF 2004-05 NATIONAL BUDGET (Presented by P. Chidambaram on 8 July 2004)

I

Mr. Speaker, Sir, I rise to present the budget for the year 2004-05. Every five years, or sometimes sooner, the people of

India speak in their collective voice. The message is usually unambiguous and clear. Elections 2004 were no different. The people's vote against one coalition—and the vote in favour of another coalition—was a vote for change. As the Prime Minister, Dr. Manmohan Singh, said in his address to the Nation two weeks ago, the people have sought "a change in the manner in which this country is run, a change in national priorities, and a change in the processes and focus of governance." I shall make every effort to be true to that mandate.

II. NATIONAL COMMON MINIMUM PROGRAMME : THE GUIDING LIGHT

The United Progressive Alliance (UPA) has given to itself, and to the people of this country, a Common Minimum Programme. The Government has since adopted it as the National Common Minimum Programme (NCMP). The programme spells out seven clear economic objectives :

- Maintaining a growth rate of 7-8 per cent per year for a sustained period;
- Providing universal access to quality basic education and health;
- Generating gainful employment in agriculture, manufacturing and services, and promoting investment;
- Assuring 100 days' employment to the bread-winner in each family at the minimum wage;
- Focusing on agriculture and infrastructure;
- Accelerating fiscal consolidation and reform; and
- Ensuring higher and more efficient fiscal devolution.

The UPA government began its journey in May this year. However, I may note that one-quarter of the year has elapsed and, by the time the Budget is passed and the President gives his assent to the Finance Bill, nearly one-half of the year will be over. There is also an Interim Budget left behind by my predecessor.

The Government has to shift gears; and even if we are able to do so quickly, it would leave us only about six months to achieve our objectives for this year. We have therefore decided to adopt an innovative approach. The Planning Commission has advised the ministries and departments to redefine their priorities and redraw their programmes in accordance with the NCMP. This will necessarily involve some changes in the allocations under each head of expenditure. Besides, new programmes or schemes may have to be launched, and old ones restructured. Under the circumstances, it was considered optimal to allow the ongoing programmes to continue until the Planning Commission completes an exhaustive review and reorients the expenditure pattern to conform to the NCMP objectives. One thing, however, is clear. The Plan resources made available in the Interim Budget will be insufficient. Hence, in addition to the Gross Budgetary Support (GBS) of Rs. 135,071 crore provided in the Interim Budget, I propose to provide a sum of Rs. 10,000 crore. This, and some other additional allocations, will raise total plan expenditure to Rs. 145,590 crore in the Budget Estimates for 2004-05.

III. FRBM AND THE MACRO-ECONOMIC BACKDROP

The Fiscal Responsibility and Budget Management Act (FRBM) 2003 has streamlined the Budget presentation process. The Government has demonstrated its commitment to prudent fiscal and financial policies by notifying the Act and the Rules with effect from July 5, 2004. Along with the Budget, a medium-term fiscal policy statement, a fiscal policy strategy statement and a macro-economic framework statement are being presented to the House.

Under the FRBM Act, I am obliged to wipe out the revenue deficit by 2007-08. However, the NCMP has proposed that we do so by 2008-09. In my view, 2008-09 is a more credible terminal year; it will also coincide with the term of this Government. Hence, I propose to move an amendment to this effect through the Finance Bill. I am committed to implementing the FRBM Act. The elimination of revenue deficit will open up fiscal space up to 3 per cent of GDP for enhanced public investment without undermining fiscal prudence.

The economic fundamentals appear strong and the balance of payments is robust. Although there are short-term pressures on prices, the outlook for the year is benign and the Government is fully alert. Growth will be sustained by increased production and value addition in agriculture, a marked improvement in industrial production, and continued buoyancy in the performance of the services sector.

The Government will follow a 5-year road map to achieve the NCMP objective of bringing about rapid growth with stability and equity. Sequencing the measures in an appropriate fashion and continuing the reform process; which ushered in the era of rapid growth, are the main challenges. The Government is committed to strike a fine balance among the three mutually reinforcing objectives of growth, stability and equity.

IV. ASSAULT ON POVERTY AND UNEMPLOYMENT

One of our greatest assets is our human resources, our people. Empowering the people, especially the poor, with universal access to education and health, and facilitating their full participation in the growth process through gainful employment, will enhance their welfare. It will also reinforce the growth process itself. This win-win strategy is the keystone of the economic policy framework of the Government.

Plan Reorientation

I have the benefit of the wise counsel of the Prime Minister, Dr. Manmohan Singh. In our scheme of things, the poor will have a first charge not only on the additional sum of Rs. 10,000 crore of GBS that I propose to provide today, but also on the entire Plan funds that the Planning Commission will reallocate.

The poor want basic education for their children : we shall provide it, and we shall make sure that the child remains in school for at least eight years. We shall also make sure that the child is not hungry while she or he is at school. The poor want drinking water : we shall ensure that every habitation has an assured source of drinking water. The poor want basic health care, medicines at fair prices and a doctor within a reasonable distance : we shall ensure that the public health system has adequate human and financial resources to provide basic medical care. The poor want jobs for their children : we shall ensure that through higher investments, and through targeted intervention, jobs are available to them.

While the Planning Commission will make the final allocations, I may assure the House that crucial programmes such as Food for Work, Sarva Shiksha Abhiyan, Mid-day Cooked-Meal Scheme, basic health care, railway modernisation and safety, Accelerated Irrigation Benefit Programme, drinking water, investment in agriculture, Provision of Rural amenities in Urban Areas (PURA), roads, and science and technology, including bio-technology, will receive priority and will be provided with additional funds.

Antyodaya Anna Yojana

I propose to continue, and expand, the Antyodaya Anna Yojana. At present, 1.5 crore families are covered. These families are provided with 35 kg. of foodgrains per family per month at a highly subsidized price of Rs. 2 per kg. for wheat and Rs. 3 per kg. for rice. 20.76 lakh tonnes of rice and 17.48 lakh tonnes of wheat were distributed under the Scheme in 2003-04. In the current year, I propose to cover 2 crore families. I expect that the off-take of rice and wheat will increase. Consequently, the Antyodaya Anna Yojana will receive a subsidy of nearly Rs. 3500 crore. A provision for this level of expenditure has been included in the allocation for food subsidy of Rs. 25,800 crore.

Public Distribution System

Fair price shops constitute the backbone of the food security system for the poor. We shall address the weaknesses in the system and strengthen public distribution. I shall return to this subject a little later.

Food for Work Programme

Investment and growth will create new job opportunities for our young men and women. Nevertheless, currently there is a need to ensure that unemployment does not take a heavy toll on the poor people. Work has begun on the National Employment Guarantee Act. The object is to guarantee 100 days of employment in a year to one able-bodied person in every poor household. The Bill will take into account the experience gained in Maharashtra. Government will also take care to avoid the pitfalls pointed out by responsible critics. My colleague, the Minister of Labour, expects that he would be able to introduce the Bill in Parliament shortly. Pending the enactment of the new law, I propose to launch a new Food for Work Programme in 150 districts classified as most backward and identified as areas in immediate need of such a programme. Allocations under different schemes will be pulled together to support the Food for Work Programme. There are substantial funds totalling over Rs. 6000 crore under SGRY, SGSY, SJSRY, REGP and PMRY. Depending on the demand for such work, more funds will be allocated in the current year. I expect to increase the allocations substantially over the next four years. Special care will be taken in laying down the guidelines for the programme so that the money and labour expended result in durable and visible assets benefiting the whole community.

Scheduled Castes and Scheduled Tribes

The welfare of the Scheduled Castes and Scheduled Tribes is close to my heart. The allocation for programmes concerning the Scheduled Castes is Rs. 1180 crore (an increase from Rs. 1137 crore) and for Scheduled Tribes is Rs. 1146 crore (an increase from Rs. 1087 crore). Other plan schemes such as SGSY, SGRY and IAY also contain specific reservations for beneficiaries belonging to the Scheduled Castes and Scheduled Tribes. The reservations range from 50 per cent to 60 per cent.

Minorities

Particular attention will be paid to the welfare, especially education, of the minorities. Hence, an additional allocation of Rs. 50 crore has been made for the National Minorities Development and Finance Corporation.

Self-help Groups

Microfinance initiatives are a cost-effective way to take the banking system to the poor. The Self-Help Group (SHG)—bank linkage programme, initiated in 1992, has come a long way. Until March 31, 2004, 1.67 crore families had benefited through 10.79 lakh SHGs financed by banks. While the SHG concept will be promoted vigorously, I am of the view that matured SHGs may be in a position to graduate from consumption or production credit to starting micro-enterprises. An indicative target of credit linking 5.85 lakh SHGs during the period up to March 31, 2007 has been set for NABARD, SIDBI, banks and other agencies.

V. THRUST AREAS

Before I deal with other areas of concern on which the Budget will have an impact, let me give you a snapshot of the goals that I have set for myself :

- Doubling agricultural credit in three years, accelerating the completion of irrigation projects and investing in rural infrastructure;
- Providing farm insurance and livestock insurance;
- Improving agricultural product markets, and promoting agri-businesses;
- Drinking water for all;
- Expanding water harvesting, watershed development and minor-irrigation and micro-irrigation schemes;
- Enhancing investment in industry—public and private, domestic and foreign—to create new jobs;
- Creating space for small-scale industry to thrive and grow;
- Electricity for all;
- Universal access to telecommunication facilities;
- More housing for the poor;
- Access to medical care through health insurance; and
- Encouraging savings, and protecting the savings of senior citizens.

I believe that the key to growth is investment—public and private, domestic and foreign. It is therefore my intention to considerably enhance investment in all sectors of the economy. However, fiscal prudence and financial discipline will remain the overarching objective. I shall also take into account the availability of resources and the absorptive capacity of various sectors.

VI. EDUCATION AND HEALTH

Education

In my scheme of things, no issue enjoys a higher priority than providing basic education to all children. The NCMP mandates Government to levy an education cess. I propose to levy a cess of 2 per cent. The new cess will yield about Rs. 4000-5000 crore in a full year. The whole of the amount collected as cess will be earmarked for education, which will naturally include providing a nutritious cooked mid-day meal. If primary education and the nutritious cooked meal scheme can work hand in hand, I believe there will be a new dawn for the poor children of India.

I am concerned about the quality of technical education in the country. Lest I be misunderstood, I am not referring to the IITs but to the ITIs. ITIs are the training ground for skilled manpower. The skills imparted by ITIs must keep pace with the technological demands of industry and the expanding universe of knowledge. There is only one benchmark for our technicians—and that is the world standard. In order to produce technicians of world standard, Government proposes to launch a programme in the Central sector to upgrade 500 ITIs over the next 5 years at the rate of 100 ITIs a year. Appropriate infrastructure and equipment will be provided, the syllabi will be upgraded and new trades will be introduced. This is an area where I welcome Chambers of Commerce and Industry to join hands with the Government and create a public-private partnership model for designing and implementing the scheme. The selection of the ITIs will be done in consultation with the State Governments.

An education loan scheme has been in operation since April 2001 under which loans up to Rs. 7.50 lakh and Rs. 15 lakh are available for professional courses within the country and abroad, respectively. The requirement of collateral was dispensed with for loans up to Rs. 4 lakh. I am happy to say that commercial banks have now agreed to waive the need for collateral for loans up to Rs. 7.5 lakh, if a satisfactory guarantee is provided on behalf of the student. Thus, no student admitted to any professional course, including courses in IITs, IIMs and medical colleges, will be deprived of the opportunity to study because of lack of funds.

Health

Access to medical care is not easily available to the poor. The Universal Health Insurance Scheme (UHIS) now in operation is skewed in favour of the non-poor. As a result, only a very small number of families below the poverty line (BPL)—actually 11,408 till May, 2004—have been covered. Although the premiums are low, BPL families seem to avoid the scheme due to their inability to pay the premium. In its present design, the scheme may not be sustainable. I, therefore, propose to redesign the scheme and make it exclusive for persons and families below the poverty line. The revised premium would be Rs. 165 for individuals, Rs. 248 for a family of five and Rs. 330 for a family of seven, without any reduction in benefits. To offset the reduction in premium, I propose to enhance the premium subsidy from Rs. 100 at present to Rs. 200 for an individual, Rs. 300 for a family of five and Rs. 400 for a family of seven. The cost to the exchequer will be Rs. 40 crore in a full year. If the money is fully spent, the number insured will rise to about 10 lakh.

In addition to the above, I propose to introduce a new Group Health Insurance Scheme through public sector non-life insurance companies. The insured will be members of Self-Help Groups (SHGs) and other credit linked groups (CLGs) who avail of loans from banks or cooperative institutions. Under the group health insurance scheme, the premium will be Rs. 120 per person, but the insurance cover would be for a sum of Rs. 10,000.

The NCMP also rightly emphasizes the need for an accelerated AIDS control programme. Bold and determined efforts need to be made to achieve zero-level growth of HIV/AIDS. These will include improved surveillance through the setting up of more sentinel sites and use of primary health centres to monitor HIV/AIDS, public awareness campaigns, promotion of safe sex through the use of condoms, prevention of drug abuse and distribution of disposable syringes. The allocation for prevention and control of HIV/AIDS is Rs. 259 crore.

VII. AGRICULTURE AND THE RURAL ECONOMY

Boosting agricultural growth through diversification and development of agro-processing is one of the objectives of the NCMP. The Prime Minister, in his address to the Nation on June 24, 2004 promised a "New Deal" for rural India. This new deal is not only essential for rural development and welfare, but also essential for achieving sustained overall annual growth of 7-8 per cent and generating employment.

The agriculture sector requires massive investments. Such investments have to be through credit-enabled private investment and enhanced public investment. I also intend to use fiscal instruments to boost investment in agriculture.

Credit

It is my intention to double the flow of agricultural credit in three years. We have made a beginning by announcing a comprehensive policy on agricultural credit on June 18, 2004. The policy has been received well and will be fine-tuned, if necessary.

Government has entrusted the implementation of the policy to the public sector and private sector banks, the regional rural banks (RRBs) and the cooperative banks.

Each RRB has a sponsor bank. I propose to hold each sponsor bank squarely accountable for the performance of RRBs under its control. RRBs that adopt a new governance standard and that abide by the prudential regulations will qualify for receiving funds from the Government for their restructuring.

The third arm for delivering farm credit is the cooperative banking system. Unless cooperative banks are healthy and creditworthy, it would not be possible to reach credit to every farmer in need of credit. The situation is grave. In order to find a durable solution, I propose to appoint a Task Force to examine the reforms required in the cooperative banking system including the appropriate regulatory regime. The Task Force will be requested to act with all deliberate speed and submit its report by October 31, 2004.

Irrigation, Rural Infrastructure

The Accelerated Irrigation Benefit Programme (AIBP) was

introduced in 1996-97 and was allotted large funds year after year. Yet, out of 178 large and medium irrigation projects that were identified, only 28 have been completed. The programme is being restructured. Truly last mile projects that can be completed by March 2005 will be given overriding priority, and other projects that can be completed by March 2006 will also be taken up in the current year. Next year we shall move the goal-post to March 2007, the year after to March 2008, and so on. I have provided a sum of Rs. 2800 crore to the AIBP this year.

The Rural Infrastructure Development Fund (RIDF) was established in NABARD in 1994-95. Five months ago, a decision was taken to close the RIDF and establish, in its place, another Fund with slightly different objectives. Many State Governments and many honourable Members have opposed the closure of RIDF. In deference to their wishes, and in tune with my own thinking, I have decided to revive the RIDF. RIDF's guidelines have been revised, and a corpus of Rs. 8000 crore will be provided for RIDF during 2004-05.

Restoring Water Bodies

I now turn to one of my big dreams. Water is the lifeline of civilization. We have been warned that the biggest crisis that the world will face in the 21st century will be the crisis of water. Water is indeed a renewable resource but, in any given year, it is not inexhaustible. The crisis of water has affected the lives of millions of our fellow citizens. In some cities, whole households keep awake to receive one or two buckets of water well past midnight. In rural areas, the girl child is often pulled out of school in order to fetch water. I am deeply concerned about the impending crisis. I therefore propose an ambitious scheme. Through the ages, Indian agriculture has been sustained by natural and man-made water bodies such as lakes, tanks, ponds and similar structures. It has been estimated that there are more than a million such structures and about 500,000 are used for irrigation. Many of them have fallen into disuse. Many of them have accumulated silt. Many require urgent repairs.

I therefore propose to launch a massive scheme to repair, renovate and restore all the water bodies that are directly linked to agriculture. In the current year, we shall begin with pilot projects in at least five districts, and we shall select at least one district in each of the five regions of the country. The estimated cost is Rs. 100 crore. Funds for the five pilot projects will be drawn from existing programmes such as SGRY, PMGJSY, DPAP, DDP and IWDP. Once the pilot projects are completed and validated, Government will launch the National Water Resources Development Project and complete it over a period of 7 to 10 years.

Funds will not be a constraint for implementing the Project. For instance, Life Insurance Corporation of India invests, on an average, Rs. 3000 crore per year in water-related programmes. I also intend to pose this Project to multilateral agencies for funding. It is my hope that by the beginning of the next decade all water bodies in India will be restored to their original glory and that the storage capacity of these water bodies will be augmented by at least 100 per cent.

Water Harvesting

Water harvesting schemes, specific to an area or village, have been found to be extremely useful. Such schemes are supported by a number of credit institutions. However, farmers belonging to the Scheduled Castes and Scheduled Tribes rarely benefit from such schemes. In order to help these farmers, Government will launch a nationwide water harvesting scheme. The scheme will cover one lakh irrigation units at an average cost of Rs. 20,000 per unit. NABARD will lend the money on easy terms and no margin money will be charged from the borrower. Government will provide a 50 per cent capital subsidy through NABARD, and the estimate for the scheme is Rs. 100 crore.

Flood Control

Thousands of lives and thousands of head of cattle are lost every year due to floods. Floods are perennial in States like Assam, West Bengal, Bihar and Uttar Pradesh. The NCMP envisages full Central support to flood control works in inter-State rivers and international rivers. The Brahmaputra Board has prepared a plan for anti-erosion and flood control works in the Brahmaputra and Barak valleys. A programme of flood control and anti-erosion will be launched in the current year. A similar programme is being implemented in the Ganga-basin

States of Uttaranchal, Uttar Pradesh, Bihar, Jharkhand and West Bengal. Rs. 30 crore has been allotted in the current year and additional funds will be provided to keep pace with the progress of works.

Diversification

India is self-sufficient in wheat and paddy but deficient in other agricultural produce. The time has come to encourage our farmers to diversify into areas such as horticulture, floriculture and oilseeds. The Anand model has been a great success in milk and milk products. Government proposes to launch a National Horticulture Mission. The goal is to double horticulture production from the current level of 150 million tonnes to 300 million tonnes by 2011-12. I invite States to join hands with the Government in launching this mission. One of the steps that States will be encouraged to take is to emulate the Anand model and establish a State Level Cooperative Society for promoting horticulture.

Oilseeds is another critical area. Last year, we produced 25 million tonnes of oilseeds, but we also imported US $ 2.5 billion of edible oil. Government will facilitate farmers to diversify into oilseeds by promoting superior seed-technology and through an appropriate policy of price support.

India must become a single market for all products, particularly agricultural produce. The existing Acts governing agricultural produce marketing committees have outlived their utility. The Government has circulated a model law. So far, ten States have initiated legal or administrative action for 'direct marketing' and 'contract farming' arrangements in line with the model law. I urge all States to enact the model law at an early date.

Research and Development

Agricultural research and development is an area which deserves special attention. The Indian Council of Agricultural Research (ICAR) is a beneficiary of the scheme under which every commercial rupee earned by ICAR, incrementally, is matched by another rupee from the Budget. Besides, ICAR receives funds from the Technology Development Board in respect of projects that are commercially viable. Agricultural research must be expanded rapidly to new frontiers such as bio-technology, vaccines and diagnostics. There must be a special focus on farming in drylands and unirrigated areas. The allocation for 2004-05 is Rs. 1000 crore (which is an increase from Rs. 775 crore in BE 2003-04), and I propose to make further allocations during the course of the year.

Agri-business

The Small Farmers Agri-business Consortium (SFAC) was set-up in 1994. Although SFAC started functioning from 1998, its corpus stands at a meagre Rs. 10.95 crore. In my view, SFAC should provide venture capital to projects and must be run, preferably by a banker, on purely business lines. The M.S. Swaminathan Research Foundation has identified 13 districts where there is a huge potential for agri-businesses and an appetite for investment of nearly Rs. 170 crore. The Ministry of Agriculture has initiated action to improve the governance of SFAC, including the appointment of a banker as the chief executive. For my part, I propose to provide the necessary additional capital that SFAC will require to aggressively promote agri-businesses.

Risk Mitigation

The Agricultural Insurance Company (AIC) was incorporated in December 2002. The National Agricultural Insurance Scheme (NAIS) which insures the yield or crop is in operation since Rabi 1999-2000. AIC is redesigning the scheme. We shall continue with the scheme and make another evaluation. Meanwhile, a pilot scheme insuring farm income (as opposed to crop) has been launched in 19 districts across 12 States during Rabi 2003-04. Government has decided to extend the scheme to Kharif 2004 in order to assess its feasibility. I wish to add that a weather insurance scheme appears to be more promising, at least in the design. AIC is introducing the scheme on a trial basis in 20 rain gauge stations in the current crop season. It is difficult to tell at this stage which of the three schemes will be successful. Agricultural insurance as well as livestock insurance are complex products and have to be designed with care. I wish to re-affirm Government's commitment to provide insurance cover to farming and livestock.

VIII. INFRASTRUCTURE

Sustainable growth depends upon the availability of efficient infrastructure. Government is committed to removing the inadequacies in infrastructure facilities through a mix of policy and fiscal measures.

Inter-Institutional Group

An Inter-Institutional Group in the power sector has succeeded in bringing 6 power projects to financial closure. Another 10 projects are on the verge of achieving financial closure. The concept can be extended to some other infrastructure sectors. I am glad to announce that IDBI, IDFC, ICICI Bank, SBI, LIC, Bank of Baroda and Punjab National Bank have formed an Inter-Institutional Group (IIG). They will pool their resources on a callable basis, and a sum of Rs. 40,000 crore will be made available as and when necessary. The IIG will ensure speedy conclusion of loan agreements and implementation of infrastructure projects. Initially, airports, seaports and tourism will be the target sectors of the IIG.

Water Supply

The Rajiv Gandhi Drinking Water Mission was intended to be implemented in the mission mode. In recent years, however, new programmes have sprung up obscuring the original mission. More than 75,000 habitations are yet to be provided adequate drinking water. Government intends to bring all drinking water schemes under the umbrella of the Rajiv Gandhi Drinking Water Mission.

The Accelerated Rural Water Supply Progamme (ARWSP) has been allocated Rs. 2610 crore in the current year. It will focus on renewal of water sources and on serving uncovered and partially covered habitations. Panchayati Raj Institutions will be encouraged to plan, implement, own, operate and maintain the rural water supply schemes in consultation with the State Governments. Funds will be devolved on Panchayati Raj Institutions to implement the ARWSP.

Likewise, the Urban Water Supply Programme is in operation in urban areas. 2151 towns qualify for consideration under the programme. In the current year a provision of Rs. 151.25 crore has been made.

The city of Chennai and other cities suffer from acute scarcity of drinking water. It is proposed to install the first large desalination plant near Chennai in the State sector, and more such plants will be installed along the Coromandel coast. A desalination plant with a capacity of 300 million litres per day (MLD) is estimated to cost Rs. 1000 crore, and there will be other costs for transmission pipelines and a captive power plant. It is proposed to implement the project through public-private partnership.

Sethusamudram Ship Canal Project

The Sethusamudram Ship Canal Project is a longstanding demand—nay dream—of the people of peninsular India. I am happy to inform the House that the Environmental Impact Assessment study of the project has been completed by the National Environmental Engineering Research Institute (NEERI), Nagpur. NEERI is now preparing the techno-economic feasibility report and the report is expected to be submitted shortly. The Ministry of Shipping proposes to establish a Special Purpose Vehicle (SPV). The SPV will raise funds for the project and Government will participate in the funding through a mix of equity support and debt-guarantee.

International Container Transshipment Terminal (ICTT) at Vallarpadam

Government attaches high priority to the development and expansion of port infrastructure. Presently, because of inadequate draft and cargo handling infrastructure, and partly due to locational disadvantages, mainline vessels often skip Indian ports. Containers from India are carried to their final destination after transshipment at Colombo, Dubai and other neighbouring ports. Kochi has locational advantages compared to other major Indian ports since it is closer to the main sea routes. Government will facilitate the construction of an International Container Transshipment Terminal (ICTT) at

Vallarpadam in Kochi port on Build, Operate and Transfer (BOT) basis.

Rural Housing

Indira Awas Yojana (IAY) has been the main instrument to provide housing to Scheduled Castes and Scheduled Tribes as well as to the non-SC/ST rural poor. Built into IAY is a credit-*cum*-subsidy scheme for rural households. A subsidy upto Rs. 10,000 and loan upto Rs. 40,000 are provided to eligible households. The allocation for IAY in BE 2003-04 was Rs. 1710 crore. In the current year, I propose to raise the allocation to Rs. 2247 crore and, if more money is needed, it will be found within the enhanced Plan outlay.

In order to complement IAY, the Golden Jubilee Rural Housing Finance Scheme was launched in August 1997 to give a boost to rural housing. The response has been encouraging, and 10.26 lakh dwelling units have been financed so far. However, the number appears to have stagnated at about 180,000 per year in the last three years. The scheme deserves a further stimulus. I am happy to announce that the National Housing Bank has offered to reduce the rate of refinance by 25 basis points this year. RBI has agreed to revise the norms of re-payment for rural housing loans by banks, so that the instalments coincide with crop cycles. A major impediment to credit for rural housing is absence of proper title to the land. The Government of West Bengal has made a law to simplify the creation of security. It appears to me that the law deserves to be emulated by other States. With these changes, I believe it is possible to set a higher target of 250,000 rural housing units per year.

IX. INDUSTRY

It is my goal to make the environment in India attractive for investors. In order to achieve that goal, I propose to establish an Investment Commission. The Commission will have the broad authority of the Government to engage, discuss with and invite domestic and foreign businesses to invest in India. It will be chaired by an eminent person. The Foreign Investment Promotion Board (FIPB) has played a useful role, and even now it serves as a one-stop centre for securing the nod of different ministries and departments to a proposed investment. Government believes that many of the functions of FIPB could be put on the automatic route, and leave FIPB as a one-stop service centre and facilitator. The function of wooing domestic and foreign investors will be performed by the proposed Investment Commission.

The government proposes to set-up a National Manufacturing Competitiveness Council. The Council will be a continuing forum for policy dialogue to energise and sustain the growth of manufacturing industries. The Council will be asked to suggest measures for enhancing competitiveness in the manufacturing sector. The Council may also recommend industry-specific or sector-specific policy initiatives to enhance competitiveness.

Foreign Direct Investment (FDI) has the potential to add a competitive edge, especially in the industrial sector. The NCMP declares that FDI will continue to be encouraged and actively sought, particularly in areas of infrastructure, high technology and exports. Three sectors of the economy fully meet this description. They are telecommunications, civil aviation and insurance. There is an urgent need for infusing huge amounts of capital in these sectors. I, therefore, propose to raise the sectoral cap for FDI in telecommunications from 49 per cent to 74 per cent; in civil aviation from 40 per cent to 49 per cent; and in insurance from 26 per cent to 49 per cent.

Capital Markets

The government is committed to the orderly development and functioning of the capital markets. A number of steps have been taken to broaden and deepen the capital markets as well as to strengthen the regulatory regime. There are some signs that retail investors are returning to the capital market. Foreign Institutional Investors (FIIs) have shown a marked preference for India over other emerging markets. In order to carry forward the process of making the Indian capital market strong and attractive, I propose to :

- Make the procedures for registration and operations simpler and quicker for FIIs;

- Raise the investment ceiling for FIIs in debt funds from US $ 1 billion to US $ 1.75 billion;
- Allow banks with strong risk management systems greater latitude in their exposure to the capital market;
- Create an alternative trading platform for small and medium enterprises (SMEs) to raise equity and debt from the capital market; and
- Initiate steps to integrate the commodities markets and the securities markets.

The RBI and SEBI will announce the necessary measures in respect of these matters. I am also happy to announce that SEBI has been able to resolve the longstanding issue of brokers' fees, and brokers may expect an announcement shortly.

Many genuine foreign institutional investors (FIIs) are professional bodies of asset managers and financial analysts who can enhance the flow of equity capital and lend depth to the capital markets. An inter-ministerial committee has recommended liberalization of FII limits in certain specified sectors. I propose to examine and implement these recommendations in consultation with the Ministries concerned.

Public Sector

The NCMP has declared the Government's policy on public sector enterprises (PSEs). While sick or ailing public sector enterprises have stirred a debate, not enough attention is paid to the healthy PSEs. I am happy to announce that in 2004-05 the Government will provide equity support of Rs. 14,194 crore and loans of Rs. 2,132 crore to Central PSEs (including Railways). Major investments will be made in PSEs falling in the sectors of power, telecommunications, railways, roads, petroleum, coal and civil aviation. I am sure Hon'ble Members will appreciate the deep commitment of Government to a strong and effective public sector operating in a competitive environment.

There is, of course, another side to the public sector. This side is beset with problems, and we must address them with responsibility and courage. Disinvestment and privatization are useful economic tools. We will selectively employ these tools, consistent with the declared policy. As a first step, I propose to establish a Board for Reconstruction of Public Sector Enterprises

(BRPSEs). The Board will advise the Government on the measures to be taken to restructure PSEs, including cases where disinvestment or closure or sale is justified.

One of our Navaratna companies, NTPC, has filed a prospectus with SEBI to raise capital through a public issue. Consequently, Government's holding in NTPC will be marginally diluted. In order to extract value for its holding and to compensate the effect of dilution, Government intends to piggy-back on the public issue of NTPC and disinvest approximately five per cent of its holding. This and some other cases which are under examination are expected to yield a sum of Rs. 4000 crore in the current year. While the disinvestment revenues will be part of the Consolidated Fund of India, I shall, while presenting the Budget for 2005-06, report to the House the manner in which the said revenues have been or will be applied for specified social sector schemes.

The NCMP contains clear policy guidelines regarding disinvestment in PSEs. As long as Government retains control over the PSE, and its public sector character is not affected, Government may dilute its equity and raise resources to meet the social needs of the people. I propose to ask the BRPSEs to examine each case objectively and make recommendations on disinvestment, consistent with the NCMP.

I am also happy to announce that I have taken the business of restructuring quite seriously. Hindustan Antibiotics Limited will be given financial support for restructuring. A rescue package has been worked out for Indian Telephone Industries (ITI), and ITI will be given Rs. 508 crore to remain out of the net of the BIFR.

Small Scale Industry

Small scale industry is, and must be regarded as, an engine of growth. At the same time SSI units must also be given the space to grow into medium enterprises. World over, policies are devised to meet the requirements of small and medium enterprises (SME). Keeping in mind the twin objectives, the Ministry of Small Scale Industry has identified 85 items that can be safely taken out of the reserved list. Furthermore, it is felt that technology upgradation of SSI units is the most urgent requirement to do business in a competitive environment. I have reviewed the Capital Subsidy Scheme, and I propose to raise the ceiling for loans under the scheme from Rs. 40 lakh to Rs. 1 crore. The rate of subsidy will also be raised from 12 per cent to 15 per cent. The scope of the scheme will be enlarged by adding more sub-sectors and technologies eligible for assistance. SSI units will be encouraged to obtain credit rating. With these measures, I expect that many more SSI units will benefit from the restructured scheme. A provision of Rs. 135.24 crore has been made for "Piomotion of SSI Schemes", and within that amount funds will be found for the Capital Subsidy Scheme.

Regeneration of Traditional Industries

Some of our traditional industries, namely, coir, handloom, handicrafts, sericulture, leather pottery and other cottage industries not only contain great potential for growth and exports, but are integral for the maintenance of our cultural heritage. Accordingly, a Fund for the Regeneration of Traditional Industries, with an initial allocation of Rs. 100 crore will be set-up. The details, including mechanism for utilization of the fund will be worked out in consultation with the industries concerned.

X. OTHER PROPOSALS

VAT

Value-added tax is a tax that has been tested and tried, and found beneficial throughout the world. The country needs a modern and efficient trade tax system that incorporates the international best practices. At the June 18, 2004 meeting of the Empowered Committee of State Finance Ministers, to which all Finance Ministers were invited, and chaired by my distinguished friend Dr. Asim Das Gupta, there was a broad consensus among the States to implement VAT. April 1, 2005 has been set as the date for implementation. I welcome the decision and warmly congratulate the State Governments. I urge all States that have not yet passed the relevant VAT legislation to do so before the end of 2004. International experience, as well as the experience of the State of Haryana, suggests that VAT will lead to an increase in revenue and not a loss in revenue. Nevertheless, in order to give comfort to the States, I propose to evolve a formula for determining the compensation for the loss of revenue, if any. I have offered the States the services of a Technical Experts Committee. The Committee will work with the States closely, and help them move steadily towards the stage of implementation.

Pension Reform

A 'defined contribution' pension scheme has been introduced with effect from January 1, 2004 for the Central Government employees recruited on or after that date. A suitable legislation to provide a regulatory framework for the scheme will be introduced in Parliament.

Export Promotion

My colleague, the Minister of Commerce and Industry, will place before Parliament by the end of this month a new trade policy. Government is of the view that Special Economic Zones (SEZs) are growth engines that can boost manufacturing, exports and employment. The private sector has shown considerable interest in the development of SEZs. Five SEZs have started functioning. SEZs require a special fiscal and regulatory regime. The Commerce Minister will, shortly, introduce a Bill for regulating Special Economic Zones, and it is my belief that the passing of such a law would be a significant milestone in our quest to become a major hub for manufacturing and exports.

Securitisation Act

The constitutional validity of the provisions of the Securitisation and Reconstruction of Financial Assets and Enforcement of Security Interest Act, 2002 has been upheld by the Supreme Court, except Sub-Section (2) of Section 17. In the wake of this judgement, many banks have pointed out practical difficulties likely to arise in speeding up the recovery of non-performing assets. It is proposed to amend the relevant provisions of the Act to appropriately address the Supreme Court's concerns regarding a fair deal to borrowers while, at the same time, ensuring that the recovery process is not delayed or hampered. Related amendments to the Recovery of Debts Due to Banks and Financial Institutions Act, 1993, if necessary, will also be made.

Interest Rates

The Central Government has saved considerably on interest on fresh borrowings because of moderate interest rates. The States were also able to borrow at lower rates and swap old high cost loans. Since 2002, States have benefited to the extent of nearly Rs. 2500 crore through the debt swap scheme. While borrowers are benefited by moderate interest rates, there is a need to boost savings and to protect the savers. I am convinced that, in the larger interests of the country, we should maintain a benign interest rate regime that appropriately balances the legitimate claims of the savers and borrowers.

I believe that all interest rates should be aligned to the market, save for one or two exceptions. There is a need for a savings instrument that will give a return to senior citizens which is above the market-determined rate. There is also a need for an instrument that will provide a risk-free avenue for all citizens to save for a longer term, and such an instrument should bear a slightly higher rate of interest. Balancing these considerations, I do not propose to make any change in the existing rates of interest on small savings instruments. Consequently, PPF, GPF and the Special Deposit Scheme will attract 8 per cent interest this year. For senior citizens, I propose to introduce a new scheme called the Senior Citizens Savings Scheme offering an interest rate of 9 per cent per annum. For all other citizens, I propose to continue the Government Savings bond which will carry an interest rate of 8 per cent per annum. The Varishta Pension Bima Yojana may no longer be necessary since the new savings scheme will cover the senior citizens adequately.

Reform of Public Distribution System

In the Tenth Plan document, the Planning Commission had suggested that a system of distributing food stamps should be tested on a pilot basis. Every eligible family will be entitled to collect its monthly quota of food stamps from a designated distribution centre, and such stamps could then be used to buy foodgrains from any food shop. I propose to introduce a pilot scheme for distributing food stamps, instead of distributing food through fair price shops, in two or three contiguous districts in a selected State. I sincerely hope that one of the States will come forward to associate with the Central Government in this experiment.

Gender Budgeting

Women's groups have met me and urged me to consider gender budgeting. This means that the budget data should be presented in a manner that the gender 'sensitivities of the budgetary allocations are clearly highlighted. An expert group on "Classification System of Government Transactions" has submitted its report on July 6, 2004. It has recommended appropriate systems for data collection and representation in the budget. The group has also recommended introduction of periodic benefit-incidence analysis. Government will examine the recommendations, and I hope it will be possible for me to implement some of them in the Budget for 2005-06.

Subsidies

Seven years ago, I placed before Parliament the first paper on subsidies. The NCMP pledges that all subsidies will be targeted sharply at the poor and truly needy like small and marginal farmers, farm labour and the urban poor. I have asked the National Institute of Public Finance and Policy (NIPFP) to prepare a blue print to accomplish these objectives. I expect to place the report before the House in the next session of Parliament.

States' Finances

In order to support the States, a substantial proportion of the taxes raised by the Central Government is transferred to the States. Besides, the Central Government extends loans to the States. In the light of the Budget Estimates for the current year, I am happy to report that the States' share of Union taxes and duties will increase to Rs. 82,227 crore from Rs. 63,758 crore in BE 2003-04. We are helping the States in other ways too. One of them is the Debt Swap Scheme. I propose to extend the facility of debt swap by allowing States to raise fresh loans and repay their old high-cost loans to NABARD and some other agencies. I also propose to consult the States on allowing them to increase their open market borrowings and reduce their dependence on loans from the Central Government. I shall also consider passing on external loans to the States on a back-to-back basis.

We are moving in the direction of empowering the States through devolution of larger resources. It is my fervent hope that States will accept the obligation to observe fiscal prudence and financial discipline.

Loans given by the Central Government to States carried an interest rate of 12.5 per cent. In 2003-04, the rate was reduced to 10.5 per cent. I am happy to announce a further reduction. Loans to the States will now bear an interest rate of 9 per cent with effect from April 1, 2004. States are expected to benefit to the tune of Rs. 375 crore this year alone.

Special Economic Packages

The NCMP promises that special economic packages for Bihar, Jammu & Kashmir and the North-Eastern States, announced in the past, will be implemented expeditiously. Bihar, for example, has a number of projects pending for a long time, including projects in power, roads, drainage and rehabilitation of displaced persons. I would like to assure the House that Bihar will be assisted through the Rashtriya Sram Vikas Yojana. A provision of Rs. 3225 crore has been made for the present and, if necessary, this sum will be augmented.

North-Eastern Region (NER)

The Government is committed to the speedy development of the North-Eastern States and Sikkim. Accordingly, all Ministries and Departments have been mandated to allocate at least 10 per cent of their Plan budget for schemes and programmes in the NER. This amounts to an allocation of Rs. 5823 crore to be spent in the NER. The amount remaining unspent from this 10 per cent allocation is transferred to a non-lapsable Central pool of resources for development of the NER. In the current year, Rs. 650 crore have been provided from the Central pool of resources for specific projects and schemes in this region, up from Rs. 550 crore in 2003-04.

Jammu & Kashmir

The Government will provide special assistance to the State of Jammu & Kashmir to have a reasonable Plan size. It will also provide financial support for the long pending Baglihar Project. The Government has also agreed to provide a grant of Rs. 300 crore to the State to ensure smooth switch-over from the current overdraft arrangement with the Bank of Jammu & Kashmir to the Ways & Means scheme of the RBI.

Backward States' Commission

NCMP envisages the creation of a Backward States' Grant Commission to be used for creating productive assets in such States. It also envisages that all non-statutory resource transfers from the Central Government will be weighed in favour of poor and backward States, but with performance parameters as well.

I am happy to announce that the Government will set-up a Backward States' Grant Fund with a corpus of Rs. 25,000 crore to be provided over a period of five years. While the existing Backward Districts Initiative Scheme with an annual outlay of about Rs. 1,800 crore will be merged into this Grant Fund, the balance amount required for the annual contribution of Rs. 5,000 crore will be earmarked from out of the total Central support to the Plan. It is expected that this will enable taking up social and physical infrastructure programmes in the poorest and most backward districts in the country within a given time frame. The Fund will become operational from the financial year 2005-06. Further details will be worked out in consultation with the Planning Commission.

Defence Modernization

As promised in the NCMP, the Government is determined to eliminate all delays in the modernization of the Defence Forces. Having regard to the trend of defence capital expenditure in recent years, it has become necessary to make a higher allocation this year. Accordingly, I propose to increase the allocation for Defence to Rs. 77,000 crore (as against Rs. 65,300 crore in BE 2003-04) which includes an allocation for capital expenditure of Rs. 33,483 crore (as against Rs. 20,953 crore in BE 2003-04).

Budget Estimates for 2004-05

Now, I turn to the budget estimates for the current year.

Plan Expenditure

While preparing the Budget, I found that there is a plethora of Plan schemes. The number, the variety and even the acronyms under which these schemes are known are mind-boggling. I also found that there are many schemes with more or less the same objectives. In some cases, all the schemes were located in one ministry or department; in other cases, they were distributed among different ministries or departments. Plan schemes can be broadly divided into three categories—Central Sector, State Sector and Centrally Sponsored Schemes. The NCMP requires that all Centrally Sponsored Schemes, except national priority areas like family planning, shall be transferred to the States. Fortunately, a new Planning Commission is in place, and I am confident that the Planning Commission will bring some order into the tangled web of schemes.

Plan expenditure for 2004-05 is estimated at Rs. 145,590 crore as against Rs. 122,149 crore in the provisional actuals for 2003-04. While there is an increase in plan revenue expenditure from Rs. 78,537 crore in 2003-04 to Rs. 91,843 crore, there is an even sharper and welcome increase in plan capital expenditure from Rs. 43,612 crore in 2003-04 to Rs. 53,747 crore.

Non-plan Expenditure

Non-plan expenditure in 2004-05 is estimated to be Rs. 332,239 crore, lower than Rs. 349,787 crore in the provisional actuals for 2003-04 which includes capital expenditure of Rs. 46,211 crore on repayment to the National Small Savings Fund. The increase in non-plan expenditure from the interim Budget is mainly on account of capital expenditure in defence (Rs. 11,000 crore), and assistance to Indian Telephone Industries Ltd.

Revenue Deficit and Fiscal Deficit

Mr. Speaker, Sir, in the Budget Estimates for 2004-05, the total expenditure is estimated at Rs. 477,829 crore, of which Rs. 145,590 crore is for Plan and Rs. 332,239 crore for non-Plan. I estimate total revenue receipts of the Central Government at

Rs. 309,322 crore and the revenue expenditure at Rs. 385,493 crore. Consequently, the revenue deficit is estimated at Rs. 76,171 crore equivalent to 2.5 per cent of GDP, which is one percentage point below the corresponding estimate of 3.5 per cent of GDP in 2003-04 (according to the provisional actuals). The fiscal deficit is estimated at Rs. 137,407 crore, which is 4.4 per cent of the estimated GDP.

XI. TAX PROPOSALS

I shall now deal with my tax proposals.

Taxation is a key tool of fiscal policy. The NCMP has promised that "tax rates will be stable and conducive to growth, compliance and investment". Thanks to policies initiated in the 1990s, direct tax rates are now moderate and require only fine tuning from time-to-time. Indirect taxes have also been moderated through a calibrated reduction in customs and excise duties. The proportion of direct tax revenues to GDP has increased from 1.9 per cent in 1990-91 to 3.8 per cent in 2003-04. As expected, the proportion of indirect tax revenues to GDP has declined from 7.9 per cent in 1990-91, but the decline has been rather sharp with the proportion at 5.3 per cent in 2003-04. The weak spot is central excise. Excise revenues are stuck, rather stubbornly, at around 3.3 per cent of GDP. While reduction in excise duty rates partly accounts for this situation, the expansion of the manufacturing industry ought to have given us larger revenues.

Through my policies on taxation, I wish to signal that we remain committed to moderation and stability in tax rates; that we remain committed to increasing revenues from direct taxes and excise duties; and that we remain committed to expanding the service tax net because the services sector accounts for 51 per cent of GDP. I shall also use tax policies to provide incentives to certain kinds of investment and to influence certain kinds of behaviour in the market.

I am a votary of tax reforms but it would be unwise on my part to attempt to do tax reform in a hurried or piece-meal manner. Seven months from now there will be another Budget, and there will be an occasion to visit the subject of tax reform.

Direct Taxes

I shall begin with my direct tax proposals. Let me give you the good news first. No one with a taxable income of Rs. 100,000 will be required to pay any income tax any more. It was not easy to reach this decision. While the tax rates are moderate, it is the tax slabs which cause concern. However, I am unable to alter the tax slabs because I cannot afford to lose a large amount of revenue at a time when the Government has assumed a larger responsibility for investment and welfare programmes. Out of nearly 3.4 crore persons filing income tax returns, only 2.7 crore assessees are taxpayers. My proposal will give relief to 1.4 crore assessees. The method that I have adopted is somewhat novel. While everyone will file his return according to the current tax slabs and tax rates, and compute his taxable income and the tax payable, any one with a taxable income of Rs. 100,000 will have his income tax liability automatically rebated. I cannot give more relief, or relief across the Board, in this Budget. If compliance improves, I promise to revisit the subject.

I propose to give relief to certain sections of deserving tax payers. Accordingly, I propose to exempt from income tax the family pension received by widows, children and nominated heirs of members of the armed forces and the paramilitary forces killed in the course of operational duties. This is my humble salute to their supreme sacrifice.

I propose to extend the benefit of Section 80DD and Section 80U in respect of persons suffering from autism, cerebral palsy and multiple disability.

Farmers have brought to my notice that agricultural land situated in certain urban agglomerations fall under the definition of capital asset and the compensation for acquisition of such land is subjected to capital gains tax. Such compensation deserves to be exempted from capital gains tax. I propose to do so in cases where the compensation or the enhanced compensation has been received on or after April 1, 2004.

A new 'defined contribution' pension scheme for new entrants into Central Government service has come into effect from January 1, 2004. The tax treatment of contributions made to the scheme has engaged the attention of Government. I propose to adopt the universally accepted formula of EET : that is, the contributions will be excluded from income for tax purposes;

the accruals will also be exempt from tax; and only the terminal benefits will be taxed at the applicable rate in the year of receipt.

I propose to withdraw a few exemptions which have outlived their utility. Interest earned from a Non-Resident (External) Account and interest paid by banks to a Non-Resident or to a Not-Ordinarily Resident on deposits in foreign currency will not be exempt from tax. Similarly, any payment made by an Indian company to acquire an aircraft or an aircraft engine on lease from a foreign state or a foreign enterprise will not be exempt from tax. These exemptions will cease prospectively from September 1, 2004.

Hon'ble Members are aware that I abolished the gift tax in 1997. That decision remains, but a loophole requires to be plugged to prevent money laundering. Accordingly, purported gifts from unrelated persons, above the threshold limit of Rs. 25,000, will now be taxed as income. Gifts received from blood relations, lineal ascendants and lineal descendants, and gifts received on certain occasion like marriage will continue to be totally exempt.

In order to promote agro-processing industries, I propose to amend Section 80IB of the Act to allow a deduction of 100 per cent of profits for 5 years and 25 per cent of profits for the next 5 years in the case of new agro-processing industries set-up to process, preserve and package fruits and vegetables.

Investment in the manufacturing sector deserves the Government's attention. Hence, I propose to continue with the additional depreciation of 15 per cent allowed under Section 32(1)(iia) on new plant and machinery acquired or installed in an existing undertaking; however, the required increase in installed capacity will now be 10 per cent, and not 25 per cent.

The automobile sector has done well and needs to be encouraged. I therefore propose to notify the automobile industry as an industry entitled to 150 per cent deduction of expenditure on in-house R&D facilities.

The power sector also deserves tax concessions. The Electricity Act, 2003 envisages unbundling of generation, transmission and distribution. In order to promote renovation and modernization of existing transmission and distribution lines, I propose to extend the benefit under Section 80IA to projects undertaken during the period April 1, 2004 to March 31, 2006.

The shipping industry has demanded the levy of a tonnage tax to make it intentionally competitive. Tonnage tax will also induce more ships to fly the Indian flag. I propose to accept the request. Consequently, the concessional regime under Section 33 AC will be withdrawn and shipping companies will now have only an option to pay the tonnage tax or normal corporate tax on profits.

I propose to extend the benefit of Section 80IB to new hospitals with 100 beds or more set-up in rural areas. Such hospitals will be entitled to a 100 per cent deduction of their profits for a period of five years.

The housing industry enjoys certain benefits under Section 80IB for projects approved before March 31, 2005. I propose to extend the time limit to March 31, 2007.

A small problem has plagued the reconstruction and development of existing buildings under approved plans in the city of Mumbai. Perhaps the problem is there in some other cities too. I, therefore, propose to relax the condition of minimum plot size of one acre in the case of housing projects, as long as the projects are implemented in accordance with a scheme for reconstruction or development approved by the Central or State Government.

Capital gains tax is another vexed issue. When applied to capital market transactions, the issue becomes more complex. Questions have been raised about the definitions of long-term and short-term, and the differential tax treatment meted to the two kinds of gains. There are no easy answers, but I have decided to make a beginning by revamping taxes on securities transactions. Our founding fathers had wisely included entry 90 in the Union List in the Seventh Schedule of the Constitution of India. Taking a cue from that entry, I propose to abolish the tax on long-term capital gains from securities transactions altogether. Instead, I propose to levy a small tax on transactions in securities on stock exchanges. The rate will be 0.15 per cent of the value of security. Thus, a transaction involving securities valued at, say, Rs. 100,000 will now bear a small tax of Rs. 150. The tax will be levied on the buyer. In the case of short-term capital gains from securities, I propose to reduce the rate of tax to a flat rate of 10 per cent. My calculation shows that the new tax regime will be a win-win situation for all concerned.

I propose to make a change in the tax on dividends distributed by mutual funds. Equity-oriented mutual funds will continue to be exempt from tax. Debt-oriented mutual funds are now required to withhold 12.5 per cent of the income distributed to unit holders. Individuals and HUF unit holders will continue to enjoy the benefit of this rate. However, in the case of corporate unit holders, I propose a rate of 20 per cent. I am sure corporates will understand, because I am doing no more than partially closing a window of arbitrage opportunity.

I propose to put an end to bonus-stripping and dividend-stripping in units by making a suitable amendment to Section 94 of the Act.

I also propose some measures to widen the tax base and to plug revenue leakage. I do not wish to take the time of the House detailing each measure.

Tax Deduction at Source (TDS) and Tax Collection at Source (TCS) are being extended to some more activities. Amendments are proposed to Section 40(a)(i) and Section 194 C.

The telecom sector enjoyed certain benefits under Section 80IA for services commenced before March 31, 2004. Pending a detailed examination of the needs of the telecom sector, I propose to extend the terminal date to March 31, 2005.

Companies carrying on scientific research and development and approved by the Department of Scientific and Industrial Research before April 1, 2004 are entitled to 100 per cent deduction of profits for 10 years. On the request of the Department of Bio-Technology and pending a detailed examination, I propose to extend the terminal date to March 31, 2005.

New industrial undertakings in Jammu & Kashmir enjoyed 100 per cent tax exemption if they commenced production before March 31, 2004. Pending a detailed examination of the incentives required to promote industrial development in Jammu & Kashmir, I propose to extend the date to March 31, 2005.

Indirect Taxes

Now, I turn to my indirect tax proposals. The policy signal

that needs to be reiterated is that customs duties will be brought down in a measured way. It is my intention to align India's tariff structure to those of ASEAN countries. Eventually, there should be a uniform rate of tax on goods and services. During the last four years, my predecessors had adjusted excise duties and moved them towards a Central VAT rate. That process must continue. The most important goods in the manufacturing sector must therefore bear an excise duty of 16 per cent.

Another principle that requires to be emphasized is that where an excise duty is levied, subject to only a few exceptions, like goods when imported should attract an equivalent countervailing duty (CVD). In my tax proposals, I have, therefore, removed the exemption from CVD enjoyed by some imported goods where there is no corresponding exemption from excise duty on Indian made goods.

I may also point out that customs tariffs and excise duties are inter-related. While considering the tax regime for any sector, one must look at both customs duties and excise duties applicable to that sector.

The peak rate of customs duty was reduced to 20 per cent in January 2004. I propose to maintain the peak rate for the rest of the current fiscal year.

I shall now deal with specific sectors beginning with metals, minerals and industrial raw materials. Steel is the leading metal. Normally, it should bear an excise duty of 16 per cent. However, in February this year, excise duty on steel was reduced from 16 per cent to 8 per cent, but with the caveat that the decision will be reviewed when the regular budget is presented. Belying expectations, steel prices have not moderated but have risen sharply. I propose to reduce the customs duty on non-alloy steel from 15 per cent to 10 per cent and to increase the excise duty on steel from 8 per cent to 12 per cent so that the countervailing duty will also be applicable to imports. I hope to recoup some of the revenue losses since February 2004.

Alloy steel, copper, lead, zinc and base metals are basic raw materials used in a variety of industries. I propose to reduce the peak rate on such metals to 15 per cent. I also propose to reduce the customs duties on refractory raw minerals and mineral products like graphite, asbestos, mica and gypsum to 15 per cent. The customs duty on all catalysts will also be 15 per cent.

I propose certain concessions to the agriculture sector. To encourage value addition, while retaining customs duty on crude palm oil at 65 per cent, I propose to accept the recommendation of the Tariff Commission and increase the duty on refined palm oil to 75 per cent.

Some items of plantation machinery attract a customs duty of 5 per cent. I propose to extend the concessional rate to more items pertaining to the tea and coffee plantation sector.

On the excise front, I propose to make a number of concessions. Tractors attract an excise duty of 16 per cent. Hereafter, tractors will be fully exempt. Likewise, dairy machinery which attracts an excise duty of 16 per cent will be fully exempt. Hand tools such as spades, shovels, sickles, etc. which currently attract a 16 per cent excise duty will also be fully exempt.

Excise duty on preparations of meat, poultry and fish will be reduced from 16 per cent to 8 per cent and excise duty on food grade hexane (used in the edible oil industry) will be reduced from 32 per cent to 16 per cent.

I propose to give some concessions to the health sector. A number of items for the disabled are already exempt from import duties or attract a concessional duty of 5 per cent. I propose that rehabilitation aids such as talking books, braille computer terminals, braille writers and typewriters, assistive listening devices, cochlear implants and stair lifts be fully exempt from customs duty. They will also be exempt from excise duty and CVD. Crutches, wheel chairs, walking frames, artificial limbs, etc. for the disabled will also be fully exempt from customs duty. There are some restrictions on institutions for the visually-impaired and the hearing-impaired availing of import duty exemptions. I propose to remove these restrictions as well as enlarge the list of exempted appliances. Ambulances used by government and municipal hospitals alone have been allowed the concessional excise duty of 16 per cent. I propose that all ambulances registered as such will be entitled to this benefit. Diagnostic kits for detecting hepatitis B alone are exempt from excise duty. I propose to extend the exemption to kits for detection of all types of hepatitis.

In order to move toward the Cenvat rate, I propose to levy excise duty on contact lenses and playing cards. I also propose to increase the excise duty from 8 per cent to 16 per cent on a few items including vaccum flasks, plastic insulated ware, scented supari, prefabricated buildings, laboratory glassware, black and white television sets, populated PCBs, imitation jewellery, candles and parts of clocks and watches. Let me hasten to add that in all these cases the general SSI exemption will continue to be available, and consumers and small manufacturers will not be affected at all. Even other manufacturers will avail of Cenvat credit.

In order to protect matches made in the non-mechanised sector, I propose to increase the excise duty on matches made in the mechanized/semi-mechanised sector from 8 per cent without Cenvat credit to 16 per cent with Cenvat credit.

The Information Technology sector has, by and large, been kept out of the reach of the tax collector. Under the Information Technology Agreement, customs duty will be brought down to zero in 2005. Meanwhile, I propose to abide by the bound rates under the agreement.

I propose to exempt specified raw materials for manufacture of parts of cathode ray tubes and specified capital goods for manufacture of mobile handsets, plasma display panels, etc. from excise duty. Specified items for manufacture of telecom grade optical fibres and cables are also proposed to be exempt from customs duty. Mobile switching centres imported by cellular mobile telephone service providers are now exempt from customs duty. I propose to extend the exemption to imports by universal access service providers.

Computers attract excise duty of 8 per cent. I propose to grant full exemption.

I propose to give some excise relief to LPG gas stoves bearing an MRP up to Rs. 2000, footwear with MRP upto Rs. 250 and writing instruments with MRP upto Rs. 200.

I propose to reduce the excise duty on amusement rides from 20 per cent to 10 per cent.

Having been Commerce Minister, export promotion is close to my heart. I propose to extend the concessional customs duty of 5 per cent on capital goods enjoyed by the leather industry to the non-leather footwear industry too.

Finished leather of all kinds is exempt from customs duty. I propose to exempt patent leather also.

Platinum is a serious challenger to gold in the jewellery industry. Both should be treated alike. Hence, I propose to reduce the import duty on platinum from Rs. 550 per 10 grams to Rs. 200. I propose that rough coloured precious gemstones should be exempt from customs duty just as rough semi-precious stones are.

Area specific exemptions from excise duty have been granted from time to time. The North-Eastern States and J & K are in a class by themselves. The exemptions enjoyed by them will continue. Sikkim, Uttaranchal and Himachal Pradesh were also granted area-based exemptions. Hon'ble Members are fully aware of the arguments in favour and the rival arguments against. I have to be fair to both sides. Accordingly, I propose that area specific exemptions enjoyed by States other than the North-Eastern States and J & K will continue and be available to units set-up or expanded on or before March 31, 2007.

I shall now deal with the most challenging tax problem that I faced this year. This relates to the textile sector. Last year, handlooms and powerlooms were brought into what is described as the Cenvat chain. The intention was good but, I am afraid, the decision did not take into account the decentralized and fragmented nature of production of fabrics in the country. Besides, the so-called Cenvat chain had nearly 40 exemptions at different stages. In fact, two exemptions were added after the decision.

I am conscious that the Agreement on Textiles and Clothing will come to an end on December 31, 2004. Our textile sector must, therefore, be made more efficient and competitive. Those who can compete because of their organizational strength should be allowed to compete; for the rest, we must allow more time to comply with a mandatory tax regime. Meanwhile, there must be a level playing field.

If I have understood correctly the mind of Hon'ble Members of Parliament, and of the leaders of various political parties, I believe that there is a universal demand to free the handloom and powerloom sectors from the Cenvat regime. After giving my anxious consideration to the complex issues, I propose to withdraw the mandatory Cenvat duty. Instead, I propose to introduce a new tax regime for the textile sector and, in this exercise, I am happy to say that I have the full support of the Minister of Textiles.

Let me now explain briefly the new regime.

- Firstly, the mandatory Cenvat chain will stand abolished.
- Secondly, there will be no mandatory excise duty on pure cotton, wool and silk, whether it is fibre, yarn, fabric or garment.
- Thirdly, blended textiles and pure non-cotton (polyester, viscose, acrylic and nylon) will have a different tax regime.
- Fourthly, there will be a mandatory excise duty on man-made staple fibre at 16 per cent; on polyester filament yarn (including textured yarn) at 24 per cent; and on other man-made filament yarn (including textured yarn) at 16 per cent.

Every manufacturer—be it handloom or powerloom or composite mill—will have the option to choose between two routes. One will be the exemption route and the other will be the Cenvat route. Under the exemption route, no excise duty will be payable at any stage (except on man-made fibre and filament yarn). Under the Cenvat route, credit can be taken for all excise duties paid at earlier stages. For the purposes of the optional Cenvat route, it is necessary to specify in the Tariff schedule the applicable excise duty rates. For the pure cotton sector, the uniform rate will be 4 per cent on yarn, fabrics, garments and made-ups. For the blended textiles sector and pure non-cotton sector, the uniform rate will be 8 per cent.

It is my firm belief that the millions of handloom weavers and powerloom weavers will welcome the new regime. As far as the composite mills are concerned, there is no cause for worry. They are also free to take the exemption route, but if they choose to opt for the Cenvat route, they may do so and claim Cenvat credit for all duties paid at earlier stages. Garment exporters should give the new regime a fair chance. I expect that prices of fabrics will moderate and garment exporters will stand to benefit. Their concerns, if any, can be addressed through the drawback or DEPB mechanism.

In course of time, it is possible that some manufacturers of handlooms and powerlooms will take advantage of the low uniform rates of duty and opt for the Cenvat route.

There remains the service tax. I propose to take a major step towards integrating the tax on goods and services. Accordingly, I propose to extend credit of service tax and excise duty across goods and services. In order to neutralize the revenue impact of such extension, and keeping in mind the mean Cenvat rate, I propose to enhance the rate of service tax from 8 per cent to 10 per cent.

58 services have been brought under the net so far. I propose to add some more this year. These are business exhibition services; airport services; services provided by transport booking agents; transport of goods by air; survey and exploration services; opinion poll services; intellectual property services other than copy right; brokers of forward contracts; pandal and shamiana contractors; outdoor caterers; independent TV/radio programme producers; construction services in respect of commercial or industrial constructions; and life insurance services to the extent of the risk premium. I may clarify that there is no intention to levy service tax on truck owners or truck operators. Nor, as was clarified by my predecessor, is there any intention to levy service tax on the savings part of the premium collected by an insurer.

I also propose that some currently taxable services should be redefined to cover all service providers falling under the same category, but I do not wish to burden this speech with the details. Exemptions granted in the case of some taxable services are proposed to be removed. The administration of service tax will be made more tax-payer-friendly. I propose to do away with the mandatory verification of self-assessment and the mandatory penalty for non-registration.

Finally, there is the tax mandated by the NCMP. That is an education cess on all taxes. I propose to levy a cess of 2 per cent on income tax, corporation tax, excise duties, customs duties and service tax.

Besides my tax proposals, I have looked at another source of revenue. There are large recoverable arrears both in direct taxes and indirect taxes. Even the undisputed arrears are quite substantial. I have, therefore, assumed that I would be able to recover a tidy sum this year. A special, multi-pronged drive will be made to recover these arrears, the details of which will be announced later.

My tax proposals on direct taxes are expected to yield a gain of Rs. 2000 crore. On the indirect taxes side, they are broadly revenue neutral.

XII. CONCLUSION

Mr. Speaker, Sir. The countries of the world, India included, have set for themselves the Millennium Development Goals. Our date with destiny is not at the end of the millennium, but in the year 2015. Will we achieve those goals? In the eleven years that remain, it is in our hands to shape our destiny. Progress is not always on a linear path, nor is it inevitable. Two thousand years ago, Saint Tirvalluvar said :

> *"Aran Izhukkathu Allavai Neeki Maran Izhukka*
> *Maanam Udayathu Arasu".*
>
> (They are good rulers who observe ethics, commit no crime and walk the path of honour and courage).

If we bring thought and passion to our governance, and walk the path of honour and courage, we can make the future happen. And this century will be India's century.

Sir, with these words, I commend the Budget to the House.

SECTION 3

COMMONMAN'S BUDGET : BUT WHERE ARE THE JOBS?

True to their philosophy, the new government of Manmohan Singh has given the nation a common man's budget where benefits announced are going to provide possible help to this person who has been a big sufferer during the past more than a decade's regime of globalisation. While cities shine with world class goods and enjoyed all around prosperity including maximum jobs created mainly in the IT and telecommunication segment where benefits have been entirely pocketed by the urbanites, the rural folks have only sulked.

Thus, it was time that development strategy took an about-turn and benefits were now focused on the rural areas.

And all this is amply reflected in the current budget where a large number of benefits have been announced to agriculture, rural development, the whole area of social development, education, public health, rural water supply, child and women welfare and several others.

After carefully scanning the lopsided development that has occurred in the rural areas, the budget has tried to restore it the honour it deserved.

It has been fully realized that if the nation were to progress effectively it could do that only through the creation of healthy rural environment, sanitation facilities, health care, education, housing facilities and other welfare schemes. And above all the creation of suitable job opportunities, which were not only sustainable but equally met with the needs of rural population, their low education and spill. That was the only way to spill prosperity at the grass-root level.

Unfortunately, this is the area which the budget has almost sidelined. It appears to have fallen in the trap that once a series of programmes were announced to bring in a new shine in the rural areas, jobs would automatically follow. Thus, there was nothing to worry about on this account.

But then the experience has shown a different picture. Jobs are not automatically created in this way. These follow a well thought out strategy where consideration is given to the various problems faced in the rural labour market, including the problems of women labour who contribute almost equally to the domestic kitty in the rural areas.

While the budget has discussed several development schemes, it has been silent on how these schemes would function to fulfil the needs of job aspirants.

For instance, there is high emphasis on rural poverty and for its wiping out massive amount has been announced. But then one doesn't know how it will be implemented for eradication of poverty. The past experience amply shows that several poverty eradication programmes that have been tried have failed to reach effectively the target groups.

A lion's share of this amount was lost in the long distribution channel. How are we going to ensure that this no longer happened and money goes straight to the poor in whatever shape it has been planned so that it benefits him and his family.

It has often been questioned that while the country has created a large stock of foodgrains and much of it is already rotting in the government godowns and even in the open space for lack of storage space and several hundred crores of rupees are being spent annually for its management and upkeep, why these stocks were not being utilized for capital formation in the rural areas.

For instance, the rural road programme on which the previous government had planned an expenditure of Rs. 60,000 crores for linking all the rural areas from one corner of the country to another, is a good instance of massive employment generation particularly for untrained and illiterate labourers who have been the worst sufferers under reforms and all of them live below the poverty line.

There is nothing new about it. Development economists have often suggested this model for developing countries starved of financial resources but having abundance of unskilled manpower. We are also faced with almost similar situation when we have a large body of illiterate and unskilled human resources soaked in poverty and the country is short of financial resources. Thus, the use of surplus manpower who have otherwise zero opportunity cost, for capital formation in rural areas is an appropriate solution for creating rural infrastructure at low cost.

And this approach would simultaneously also help the country to get rid of excess food stocks which are not only imposing a high cost of stocking and look after but also there is danger that in case these were not disposed early they might become unfit for human consumption.

Further when we talk of compulsory schooling for making the entire population literate, we hardly give serious thought to why a large number of children are not attending school and even those who attend there is a high rate of drop-out. It is mainly because of the fact that their parents need them to contribute to the meager family kitty to save them from starvation. It is all the more so in case of girls who hardly attend school.

Thus the disgusting situation in rural education is due to the lack of employment avenues which would provide regular income to these families. If these were there, there is no reason why children didn't attend school or dropped half way. So there is a strong need for creating employment avenues in the first instance before any thing else and there could not be better employment creating channel than capital formation through human labour.

6

Seven Pillars of Development

OBSERVATIONS

After Manmohan's historical speech on the Independence Day, my brother-in-law from Amritsar rang me up to tell that among all the Independence Day Speeches he has listened for the past several years, none could match the one delivered by Manmohan Singh. It was straightforward, plain and no hanky-panky. Manmohan had admitted he was not here to make false promises to the nation, though he was fully conscious of the fact that his government has to do a lot to improve the status of the common man.

While going through the long speeches delivered by most of the leaders on early occasions we find that these had often highlighted a number of promises made where several of these were soon forgotten and even those that were tried several of them had failed to take off. Thus, people had been fed on false promises, a political stunt to win over heir favour.

Fortunately there is nothing of this sort in Manmohan's agenda. He is a plain man, speaks out what is feasible without beating about the bush. Often he seeks the cooperation from other parties for the smooth functioning of the government.

Thus unlike most other politicians, there is no double-speak in his speech. He means what he says. He doesn't believe in misleading the nation. Soon the people will start realising this trait in him. It is probably for the first time in the post-Independence history of this country that truth has begun to take the front seat.

Simultaneously, however, a question also arises, will those in the opposition who are ever prepared to put down the functioning of the present government, even try to label it as a non-functioning government and also don't mind adding in the same breath that it was functioning against the interest of the common man and so on—allow this government to have an easy time?

Thus, instead of keeping quiet or ignoring the opposition's wrong signals, Manmohan's government should condemn it in a strong language and simultaneously quicken the pace of promised programmes for ultimately it is through the positive achievements that they would be able to silence the voice of dissidents and electorates would thus be no longer fed on the false propaganda of the opponents as they would now know the correct position.

In other words, development has to take its shape in concrete terms around the seven-point programmes, about which Manmohan talked so much on the Independence Day—viz., agriculture, water, education, health care, employment, balanced urban growth and infrastructure.

He emphasised that these were the seven pillars around which the fast development of the country would centre. Initially their benefit would flow more into the rural societies to close down development gap that has fast arisen here compared with urban areas. Ultimately, there would emerge a more balanced rural-urban development.

Thus the Independence Day speech by Manmohan Singh has made a healthy start of the Common Minimum Programme of the present government.

PRIME MINISTER MANMOHAN SINGH'S ADDRESS ON THE 58TH INDEPENDENCE DAY, AUGUST 15, 2004

"For the struggle they waged under the inspiring leadership of Mahatma Gandhiji and for the victory they won against foreign rule. This is a day we thank our soldiers and security forces for their bravery and commitment. We salute them for their dedication and discipline—farmers, workers, teachers, professionals, scientists and our elected representatives.

"In every walk of life, each one of us contributes in our own way to the building of our dear *Bharat*. What is that *Bharat* that we all wish to build?

A *Bharat* that is just and humane.

A *Bharat* that treats all its citizens as equals.

A *Bharat* that is prosperous.

A *Bharat* that lives in peace.

A *Bharat* in which every person is literate and healthy.

A *Bharat* in which everyone who seeks work is able to find it, and works for a brighter future for all of us. My greetings to all of you.

"As I stand here before you, I am reminded of the words of our first Prime Minister Pandit Jawaharlal Nehru, when he spoke to the Nation on the first anniversary of our Independence in 1948. At that time I was a young student, and looked upon the dawn of Independence as the opening up of new vistas of opportunities to build an India of our dreams. Panditji had then said, "All of us talk of India and all of us demand many things from India. What do we give her in return?" Panditji asked, and he said, "India will ultimately give us what we give her of love and service and productive and creative work. India will be what we are : our thoughts and actions will shape her.

"Friends, I ask each one of you to remember these wise words of Panditji as you go about doing your work, be it on farms, in factories, in schools, in colleges, in government offices, in shops, in research laboratories. Our Nation is what we are. It will become what we make of ourselves.

"Brothers and sisters, it is one brick after another that helps make a building. Millions of bricks go to make a great building.

In the same manner, the efforts of millions of people go into the formation of a nation. The process of nation-building is a great enterprise of adventure and creativity. It requires all of us to work together, bonded by our love for our Motherland. This love flows from our identity as Indians. Whatever be our religion, region, language, caste or culture, we are all Indians and India is ours.

"Our strength derives from our unity in diversity. The principles of secularism, social justice and the equality of all before law are the defining feature of our nation. Today is a day we re-dedicate ourselves to the service of our Nation, and of each and every citizen, especially those less fortunate than us.

"This day comes for us in the middle of the monsoons. Each year when we meet here and see the *Tiranga* being unfurled on the Red Fort, we also look at the clouds above and wonder whether it would rain. This year too we have looked at the skies with anxiety.

"In Andhra Pradesh I went to understand the problems of farmers, suffering from the impact of drought, and to hold the hands of the families that had lost their breadwinner due to the unbearable burden of debt. For miles together I could see no water. In Assam and Bihar I went to share the concern of people whose lives have been dislocated by floods. For miles without end I could see only water. Drought and floods are two fundamental problems that continue to bring suffering to our rural population. We need concerted action to deal with these perennial problems.

"Our government has already taken some steps to deal with them. We intend to take more steps in future. We need to insulate our people from the impact of drought by creating local level water security. We have to mobilize our people to come forward to take up the challenge of water conservation and management. We are committed to increasing public investment in irrigation and addressing the specific problems of each river basin, in an environment and people friendly manner.

"Water is a national resource, and we have to take an integrated view of our country's water resources, our needs and our policies and water utilization practices. We need to ensure the equitable use of scarce water resources.

"The waters of our sacred rivers have for centuries nurtured our civilization. They are the threads that run through the fabric of our nation. We cannot allow these waters to divide us. I urge you and all our political leaders to take a national and a holistic view of the challenge of managing our water resources.

"Dealing with the problem of water is an important commitment we have made as part of our "New Deal for Rural India". We have also taken steps to address the problem of availability and access to credit in rural areas. The "New Deal" that rural India needs must encompass investment in irrigation, credit delivery, health care, availability of electricity, primary education, rural roads and the modernization of the infrastructure for agriculture.

"We must increasingly use modern science and technology to address the needs of dry land farming, the diversification of our cropping pattern, micro-irrigation and the quality of our livestock. Improving rural connectivity and access to information can enrich the farm community. Here Governmental initiative can be multiplied by the effort of private enterprise and community action.

"Friends, more than three decades ago, Smt. Indira Gandhiji had given the call "Garibi Hatao". We have reduced the incidence of poverty to some extent, but there is much more remaining to be done. While liberalizing and modernizing our economy and enabling individual enterprise to blossom, we must pay special attention to the elimination of poverty and the empowerment of Scheduled Castes, Scheduled Tribes, Other Backward Castes and minorities. Our development strategies for tribal areas must be adequately sensitive to their felt needs and aspirations.

"The empowerment of women is an important priority and the education of the girl child is vital to it. Our children are our future. In framing our policies we must keep the interests of future generations in mind. The Government will pursue social and economic policies that are conducive to the proper growth and development of our children, investing in their education, health and nutrition. A healthy child makes a healthy nation.

"Employment generation has not kept pace with demand for jobs. Government will address this deficiency in the growth process by encouraging the growth of small and medium enterprises, agro-industries and sectors like tourism, where there is a high job potential. There is also an urgent need to provide employment in rural areas especially in areas suffering from prolonged drought. The "Food For Work Programme" will be an important part of our strategy to deal with this challenge. New investment in the infrastructure sector will also help generate new jobs.

"Our approach has to be one of seeking faster growth while ensuring that the benefits of growth are more evenly distributed. Our policies for higher economic growth and modernization will be combined with an emphasis on social justice, communal harmony, rural development, regional balance and concern for the environment.

"Dear Countrymen, from the National Common Minimum Programme, I have identified seven priority sectors for focused attention. These are agriculture, water, education, health care, employment, urban renewal and infrastructure. These Seven Sectors (*saat sutra*) are the pillars of the development bridge we must cross to ensure higher economic growth and more equitable social and economic development.

"The concerns of most of our citizens revolve around what we do for agriculture, water, education, health and employment. We recognize that for the development of the country what we are able to do in the key infrastructure sectors like power, roads, railways, ports and airports is also critical.

"The plans and priorities of our government have been outlined in detail in the National Common Minimum Programme, in my first address to the nation and in the Finance Minister's recent Budget speech. Today, I have no promises to make, but I have promises to keep.

"The real challenge for me and for the Government at all levels is the challenge of implementation of our stated policies and programmes. Central, State and local bodies have to work together for Government to be an effective instrument of development for the benefit of our people. There are areas, in which the Government has to be actively engaged, like education, health care, roads, railways, high technology and defence.

"However, for Government to be able to deliver results, we must reform the functioning of government. We have to make officials accountable—make Government more transparent. We have to make public enterprises more efficient. Citizens increasingly demand governments that are accountable to them. They have a concern both for probity and efficiency in public affairs.

"Fellow Citizens, the question of ethics in public life has repeatedly agitated our people and we have tried to find Constitutional, legislative and administrative devices to deal with the challenge. The time has come for us to consensually evolve a code of conduct for all political parties, a code of ethics for all individuals in public life, and a code of best practices for the Government at all levels. On this solemn occasion let us resolve to work together to develop such a code of conduct in a consensual way so as to uphold the values enshrined in our Constitution.

"We must also look within our parties, and ourselves and ask ourselves what is the root cause of the decline in values in public life? How do we reform our public institutions, our political parties, and our government at various levels? When we launched economic reforms over a decade ago, we tried to liberate individual enterprise from the stranglehold of bureaucracy. We will continue to widen the space available for private enterprise and individual initiative.

"But governments cannot be wished away, especially in a developing country like ours where the government has an important role to play. The challenge for economic reform today is to breathe new life into government so that it can play a positive role where it must.

"But what is government? Government comprises people's representatives and civil servants. The reform of government is, therefore, a reform of the way we, the elected representatives and officials, work in government. It is you, fellow citizens, as members of the civil society, who must mobilize your enormous resources in support of such reform. To make democratic institutions more accountable we are committed to take several steps to strengthen the lowest tier of panchayats and urban local bodies. We need to build the capacity of decentralized bodies and their elected representatives and this is best done through effective transfer of funds and functions to them.

"Today if we effectively utilize our decentralised system of governance through Panchayat Raj, we can take concerted action for more effective delivery of basic services such as primary education, public health and health care, providing safe drinking water and sanitation.

"When we talk of reforming government and of Panchayat Raj we are reminded of Rajiv Gandhi who took pioneering initiatives in both these areas. Also, nearly twenty years ago, Rajiv Gandhi first drew the nation's attention to the newly emerging electronics and computer revolution then underway. The enthusiastic manner in which the young people of our country have participated in the information technology revolution, turning India into an "IT super power", is a tribute to the farsightedness of Rajivji.

"It is a matter of satisfaction today that IT is enabling us to improve the standard of living of ordinary people even in remote areas. We will continue to explore ways in which modern technology can improve the lives of ordinary people. We will improve broadband access and enable the required investment in IT infrastructure.

"We live in an age where science and technology have become an important determinant of power and wealth. For our country to attain its due place in the 21st century, it is necessary to integrate science and technology in to all our development processes. The promotion of scientific temper must truly become a massive national movement.

"We cannot make higher education a prisoner of either bureaucracy or ideology. It must develop on the foundations of professional excellence and intellectual integrity. The pursuit of excellence and concern for social equity must inform all our educational processes. The revered Dr. Ambedkar recognized very early the importance of education in the empowerment of the under-privileged. "We may forego material benefits", observed Dr. Ambedkar, "but we cannot forego our right and opportunities to reap the benefit of the highest education to the fullest extent."

"Dear Countrymen, ours is a vast country in which many States are as big as some countries of the world. For the benefits of development to reach all corners of the country the Centre and States have to work in a spirit of cooperative federalism. It is the responsibility of the central government to help States to realize our common and shared objectives of development. But, there is much that State and local governments can do to promote growth, social justice and welfare. They must raise the required resources to the extent feasible. Equally important, attention must also be paid to the quality and effectiveness of Government.

"I am concerned about the slow rate of growth of the backward regions, just as I am concerned about the economic distress of the less privileged sections of our society.

"We will encourage new investment in less developed regions. We will help in strengthening developmental institutions there. Special attention must continue to be paid to governance and development in the North-Eastern States and in Jammu and Kashmir. The pattern of development must be such as to create new opportunities for job creation so that the youth of these regions can look to the future with renewed hope and confidence. These regions of our country can benefit by improving rail and road connectivity and encouraging new investment.

"Both the North-East and Jammu and Kashmir are the most beautiful regions of our country. If we can work together to create an environment conducive to development and tourism, these regions will prosper more. Peace, social and political stability and communal harmony are essential for economic development. People want such peace and stability so that they can lead safe, secure and normal lives and go about their work, relax and enjoy life.

"We must fight all anti-national and anti-social forces that try to disrupt normal life. Be they terrorists or communal and other such divisive forces. Terrorism is a threat to our normal lives and we must all unite in fighting it. Violence has never helped in the progress and prosperity of any society. We will fight this menace to civilized existence with determination. There should be no doubts on this score. However, we are willing to talk to any group provided they abjure the path of violence.

"Friends, today I want each of you to show the same degree of self-confidence that our freedom fighters showed, when they led our country to freedom, in your encounters with new markets and new opportunities. We have been an open society. But, in being open to the world, we have not lost our identity as a people. Again I remind you of what Gandhiji taught us. That our nation must be like a house built on firm foundations, whose windows are wide open to let the winds blow freely in every direction.

"I want the winds from every corner to blow through my house" Gandhiji said, "but I refuse to be swept-off my feet by any of them". That has been our attitude to the world, culturally and economically, for centuries. We must continue to adopt that attitude even as we seek to build a more self-reliant and modern economy.

"It is such focused attention to development that will address the real concerns of our people today. It is by strengthening our economy and making our democracy more inclusive that we can walk tall in the comity of nations. It is because of our commitment to democracy and development that we also wish to live in peace in our neighbourhood and with the world as a whole.

"As a people we have always lived in peace with our neighbours in Asia and the Indian Ocean region. For centuries we welcomed with open arms both travellers and traders from different parts of the world. We ourselves set sail in search of markets and to spread the philosophies of our wise men. Even today we want to live in a neighbourhood of peace and prosperity.

"I assure our armed forces and security forces our unstinted support to their welfare and to the modernization of our defences. They have played an admirable role in the defence of our unity and integrity. Not only have they defended our frontiers but also at home they have readily helped whenever their services have been sought in rescue and relief operations and in the protection of the life and property of fellow Indians.

"Even as we devote our attention to defence, we must pay heed to the needs of development. All our neighbours are, like us, developing countries whose priority will also have to be the improvement of the quality of life of their citizens. We are not only bound together by our common borders but also by our common destiny. The assurance of peace and prosperity in our neighbourhood is an important priority for us. Our Government will give the highest priority to building closer political, economic and cultural ties with all our neighbours.

"We have always been in favour of a purposive bilateral dialogue with Pakistan to resolve all outstanding issues. It is our intention to carry forward with firm resolve and sincerity the composite dialogue process with Pakistan. The edifice of peace that we wish to build must stand on the twin pillars of mutual trust and confidence. Of course, trends of cross-border terrorism and violence make our task more difficult and complex.

"As far as our relations with China are concerned, the positive trends which commenced with Shri Rajiv Gandhi's visit to China in 1988, have provided a sound basis for later trends in our bilateral ties. We are committed to strengthening and expanding these relations. We shall carry forward the process of discussion to resolve the boundary question with political vision and a practical approach.

"We value the friendship of all nations, big and small and we will seek closer economic relations with all countries. As a democratic country of more than a 100 crore people we are destined to play an important and positive role in world affairs, in structuring a just international order.

"As a people, Indians have contributed a great deal to the advancement of knowledge. We value the positive role that the people of Indian origin have played in other countries. People of Indian origin are our cultural ambassadors wherever they live. We value their contribution to the societies they now live in just as much as we value the contribution they make to India, the land of their ancestors. Indians abroad are our "Brain Bank". They have shown how enterprising we Indians can be if the environment is conducive. If the required infrastructure is provided and individual initiative is rewarded we can be as good as the best in the world.

"At home, this is the challenge for our Government. To create the environment in which merit is recognized, hard work and creativity are rewarded.

"My dear countrymen, brothers and sisters, there are many things we must do in government to be able to meet your needs and fulfil your aspirations. This is a responsibility we have taken upon ourselves and as your representatives in government we are ultimately answerable to you. This is the essence of a democracy and I have accepted this responsibility with all humility.

"The power of the people, however, is infinitely greater than the power of governments. But, it is by combining the two that we can make our nation truly great. However, as I have said already, there are limits to how much the government can do. Part of the solution lies in each one of us, in our families, in our communities. If we can all cooperate with one another and work together as a community there is much we can do without looking for intervention by the government. We have to revive the spirit of community service and the spirit of nationalism, especially among our youth.

"Our national movement is unique in world history because we secured our freedom through non-violent means and by igniting hope in the minds of ordinary people. Generations of young people have been inspired by the Mahatma, a frail and soft-spoken man who shook the foundations of the mighty British Empire.

"I want our youth to understand Mahatma Gandhiji's message that each one of us has the power to do good for our nation if we are only so determined. Let us all work together to revive that spirit of idealism, self-sacrifice, discipline and unity of purpose that characterized our freedom struggle. I am confident that the people of this great nation have the will, determination and the resources to meet this challenge. India's destiny beckons us to pool all our wisdom, experience and knowledge to make this future happen.

"I am confident that this is possible and within our reach. Our government will do all that lies within its power to convert this dream into a living reality so that this ancient land of Bharat once again becomes a major powerhouse of both knowledge and creativity. I commit our government to the fulfilment of this sacred national task."

7

Common Minimum Programme : A Close Look

This chapter is divided into two sections. Initially we have a review of main areas of Common Minimum Programme (CMP) of the present government. In Section 2 the text of Common Minimum Programme is reproduced.

SECTION 1

OBSERVATION ON COMMON MINIMUM PROGRAMME

The CMP lists a series of programmes to which attention would be given by the new government. These programmes have been prepared after the agreement reached by the supporting political parties. Its major emphasis is on employment, agriculture, rural development, education, rural infrastructure and social development. One could say it puts special emphasis on the overall rural development through a series of programmes in order to bring this neglected homeland of two-thirds of the country's population on the path of development within a period of five years. Ultimately they would be brought close to urban areas which have been shining under globalisation.

Employment appears to occupy a high priority. It is clearly laid down that at least one earning member in each family would be provided minimum of 100 days of employment in a year. One hopes it is not a vague commitment like in the past. Even so, a few question arise. It is not specified what would be the type of programmes, whether employment would bring sufficient income to sustain a family even during this time. Then the major question is how about the rest of the period? Perhaps it is thought that for this period the family would be able to find alternative employment.

Unfortunately we have failed to grasp the fact that rural employment can't be sustained on uncertain doles. It should be therefore our goal to ensure that at least one earning member in a family has employment for the full year and then at an income level which provides decent living to the family.

Though it is an Herculean job, it could be achieved through tapping properly the vast opportunities available in the rural capital formation programmes.

Agriculture

Next agriculture has turned out to be another key area on which a large emphasis has been laid. Here rightly a large dose of investment is proposed to be made on research and irrigation.

Green revolution in Punjab owes much to research and the creation of proper infrastructure. Punjab Agriculture University has played an important role in this revolution. But then over time it has failed to make similar contribution in other areas to sustain Punjab's high place in agriculture.

In fact over the last decade the traditional crops of wheat and rice continue to be in the frontline of the farmers' kitty resulting in high growth of their stocks in private and government godowns and much of it is unfortunately rotting for the lack of demand. It is regrettable that simultaneously the economy has failed to develop diversification of farm economy.

In other words, farm scientists have failed to develop high yielding varieties in those crops which could have replaced excess production in wheat and rice and also saved it from high pollution of atmosphere basically because of excess rice cultivation depending on underground water sources.

Further the earlier zeal of involvement of PAU and other farm scientists in agriculture research is lacking now. Also it has been observed that farm scientists in general have failed to interact with farmers and prefer confine themselves to the four walls of their rooms writing research papers for foreign journals in the hope of making their presence in foreign countries.

Thus, research is mainly used to enhance personal gain of scientists and develop links with foreign countries. In case we want research to serve the needs of the country, farm scientists would have to change their mind set and like earlier period renew their contacts with farmers and listen to their problems and provide them with appropriate guidance.

So care should be taken that research becomes purposeful and no longer confined to labs or used for personal gain of scientists.

Manpower in Agriculture

It is also essential that manpower depending on agriculture is drastically reduced and instead of two-thirds of population depending on agriculture as it is the case at present the future is brought down to one-third. In other words, around 30 per cent of the farm population should be depending on alternative activities.

This would also help better utilization of manpower in agriculture. Also the experience of developed countries tells that it is through advancement of farm technology, infrastructure and markets that lesser and lesser of manpower is needed to work on farms.

But then the question arises, how this is too achieved and where would the excess manpower go? So attention shifts to farm-related alternative activities like agri-processing, fruit-processing, vegetable growing, mushroom cultivation, floriculture and a host of other farm-based activities.

Thus if we want the excess manpower on the farm sector is to be reduced, it is the development of small and medium industries mostly farm-based which would have to take up an important role in the rural economy.

Rural Industrialisation

Thus ultimately rural economy has to turn to a large scale industrialisation which would call for the presence of basic facilities like infrastructure, trained labour, markets. Thus instead of laying emphasis on eight years of compulsory school, as suggested in their programme by the new government, it would be more appropriate if major emphasis is laid on vocational education. That would help us to have the needed manpower for rural industrialisation and services.

Among industries, agri-industries should constitute the central place in the strategy of small industries. In fact when we diversify agriculture, several processing industries would emerge which should be developed on a scientific basis. While the country has a large scope for agri-industries, these have yet to emerge. It is found that barring a few large units, agri-industries are yet a taboo for medium and small units.

Apart from non-availability for suitable technology we don't have sufficient market for agri-industries products. It is the quality of agri-industries products and their acceptability by consumers which should occupy the key position in these industries. That's where small even medium units have found it difficult to compete.

Thus if the growth of these industries is to proceed on a scientific basis they should have access to the latest technology, skills and market opportunities where a lot of homework was needed. A part of research programme should be devoted to these industries which would bring a good rewards. In fact in all the key villages there should be special area earmarked for the development of various agri-industries, where they should have access to modern technology, required inputs, training programme, marketing and other facilities.

Education

A large emphases in the CMP has been out on education where liberal funds would be available through a special cess of two per cent to be levied on all the Central taxes. There is also compulsory education for all children for eight years. As mentioned earlier, education would be more meaningful if it were by and large integrated with vocational education.

Further the present high rate of drop-outs is a discouraging feature. It shows that either the current mode of education holds no attraction and does not appeal to the rural children or else it is due to economic compulsion where the foremost concern for the rural household is to have sufficient income to keep the spectre of hunger away from their door. Thus they are forced to withdraw children to add to the family income. This is a highly discouraging sign for the spread of education among children. Under the circumstances one also wonders how the proposed eight-year compulsory education programme would work.

We should find a way out for this. Earlier we have suggested that the start of the rural capital formation programmes would encourage the flow of regular income to rural households. Thus, there would be no longer the need to withdraw children to add to the family income.

Therefore, regular income programmes for the rural adults would be the best remedy for their children to take advantage of school education under the new programme for eight years of schooling where with emphasis on vocational education we would also be creating skilled manpower to work in a host of activities that are going to be created now. So the changed system of school education would result ultimately in long-term multiple growth programmes in rural areas, bringing them the urban areas.

Social Development

A large emphasis is also laid on the creation of a host of social facilities in the rural areas. Currently one is baffled with the fact that doctors are not prepared to work in the rural areas. They think that rural posting is a punishment posting where they don't have anything of interest which they find in abundance in urban areas.

Thus the best solution for this sort of problem is to create urban facilities in rural areas which would not only help doctors, even other professionals like teachers. Also there is the basic question, why should we need a highly qualified professional for the rural areas? Why not create intermediate level of professionals, needing short duration and less expensive courses?

Here we could benefit from the Chinese example of 'barefoot doctor' a term used for doctors working the rural areas. They hail mostly from rural areas and are created after a simple study course but more emphasis is laid on practical training which serves well the needs of rural population. The biggest advantage of this system is that these 'barefoot doctors' being rural-based are available to the villagers for 24 hours, unlike the city bred highly qualified doctor.

Infrastructure

Infrastructure programme like roads, irrigation, power, water supply, sanitation etc., constitutes an important area of rural development and also has the biggest rural employment potential. In fact, the previous government had budgeted a sum of 60 thousand crores for rural roads which would link every rural area in this country.

It is also on the development of rural infrastructure that the overall development of the national economy results. Whether it is agriculture or small industries or rural services, the lack of infrastructure facilities acts as a major handicap to the overall development. In fact, one would not hesitate to add that it is the growth of proper infrastructure facilities that would bring rural areas close to urban areas and thus it acts as a major catalyst for the overall growth of the economy.

Urban Development

While rural development is the major focus of the present government, at the same time they have not withdrawn from urban development. In fact, it would be suicidal to do so when it has been the urban development that has changed a lot of urban economy.

The government is quite conscious of the role played by the urban development under globalisation, the inflow of foreign investments in critical areas and the help rendered by foreigners in several consumer and capital industries, and there has been high growth in IT and telecommunication facilities where India has emerged as one of the top destinations.

The various handicaps faced by the urban development would also be looked into carefully and high investment syndrome would continue to be encouraged. In fact, the contribution of the urban sector would in no way be less to the country's economy.

The only difference now is that the rural development which was so far low key area of growth would now move to the path of high growth. That is the basic philosophy behind Common Minimum Programme.

SECTION 2

COMMON MINIMUM PROGRAMME

Common Minimum Programme under the leadership of Sonia Gandhi was endorsed by all the members of United Progressive Alliance (UPA). Sonia Gandhi will herself monitor the implementation of the CMP. She will head the 12 member advisory panel, with senior cabinet rank and legal endorsement, to monitor and implement the CMP.

Highlights of CMP

- Economic growth target of 7-8 per cent per year.
- Legal guarantee for 100 days of employment.
- Cess on all central taxes.
- Disinvestment Ministry to be scrapped.
- Profit-making PSUs not be privatised; Navratnas to be retained.
- FDI to be encouraged in infrastructure, high-technology and exports.
- Labour laws to be re-examined.
- VAT to be introduced.
- Special schemes to unearth black money.
- SEBI to be further strengthened.
- Integrated energy policy; energy security to be enhanced.
- A National Manufacturing Competitiveness Council to be set-up.
- Strengthening of public distribution system.
- Review of Electricity Act, 2003.
- Protect national interest of farmers at WTO; play proactive role in G-20.
- Trade and investment with China to be enhanced.
- Bill for one-third reservations for women in Assemblies and Lok Sabha.
- Bill to repeal POTA.
- Bill on domestic violence and against gender discrimination.
- Bill to give women equal rights of ownership of assets like houses and land.

- Immediate introduction of Bill on National Employment Guarantee Act.
- A model comprehensive Bill to deal with communal violence.
- Respect Article 370 giving special status to Jammu and Kashmir.
- Amend labour laws to protect workers against "hire and fire" policy.
- Amend the Constitution to establish a Commission for Minority Educational Institutions that will provide direct affiliation for minority professional institutions to central universities.

Complete Text of CMP

Following is the text of the Common Minimum Programme of the United Progressive Alliance released in New Delhi on 27th May, 2004.

Introduction

The people of India have voted decisively in the 14th Lok Sabha elections for secular, progressive forces, for parties wedded to the welfare of farmers, agricultural labour, weavers, workers and weaker sections of society, for parties irrevocably committed to the daily well-being of the common man across the country.

In keeping with this mandate, the Congress, its pre-poll allies that include the RJD, DMK, NCP, PMK, TRS, JMM, LJP, MDMK, AIMIM, PDP, IUML, RPI(A), RPI(G) and KC(J) have come together to form a United Progressive Alliance (UPA). The UPA government supported by the Left Parties will have six basic principles for governance.

- to preserve, protect and promote social harmony and to enforce the law without fear or favour to deal with all obscurantist and fundamentalist elements who seek to disturb social amity and peace;
- to ensure that the economy grows at least 7-8% per year in a sustained manner over a decade and more and in a manner that generates employment so that each family is assured of a safe and viable livelihood;

- to enhance the welfare and well-being of farmers, farm labour and workers, particularly those in the unorganized sector and assure a secure future for their families in every respect;
- to fully empower women politically, educationally, economically and legally;
- to provide for full equality of opportunity, particularly in education and employment for scheduled castes, scheduled tribes, OBCs and religious minorities; and
- to unleash the creative energies of our entrepreneurs, businessmen, scientists, engineers and all other professionals and productive forces of society.

The UPA makes a solemn pledge to the people of our country: to provide a government that is corruption-free, transparent and accountable at all times, to provide an administration that is responsible and responsive at all times.

Employment

The UPA government will immediately enact a National Employment Guarantee Act. This will provide a legal guarantee for at least 100 days of employment to begin with on asset-creating public works programmes every year at minimum wages for at least one able-bodied person in every rural, urban poor and lower middle-class household. In the interim, a massive food-for-work programme will be started.

The UPA government will establish a National Commission to examine the problems facing enterprises in the unorganized, informal sector. The Commission will be asked to make appropriate recommendations to provide technical, marketing and credit support to these enterprises. A National Fund will be created for this purpose.

The UPA administration will revamp the functioning of the Khadi and Village Industries Commission (KVIC) and launch new programmes for the modernization of coir, handlooms, powerlooms, garments, rubber, cashew, handicrafts, food processing, sericulture, wool development, leather, pottery and other cottage industries.

The UPA government will give the highest investment, credit and technological priority to the continued growth of agriculture, horticulture, aquaculture, floriculture, afforestation, dairying and agro-processing that will significantly add to the creation of new jobs.

Along with vastly expanding credit facilities for small-scale industry and self-employment, the UPA government will ensure that the services industry will be given all support to fulfil its true growth and employment potential. This includes software and all IT-enabled services, trade, distribution, transport, telecommunications, finance and tourism.

The textile industry will be enabled to meet new challenges imposed by the abolition of quotas under the international multi-fibre agreement in January 2005. Given its special ecological importance world-wide and within the country, the jute industry will receive a fresh impetus in all respects.

Agriculture

The UPA government will ensure that public investment in agricultural research and extension, rural infrastructure and irrigation is stepped up in a significant manner at the very earliest. Irrigation will receive the highest investment priority and all on-going projects will be completed according to a strict time schedule.

The rural co-operative credit system will be nursed back to health. The UPA government will ensure that the flow of rural credit is doubled in the next three years and that the coverage of small and marginal farmers by institutional lending is expanded substantially. The delivery system for rural credit will be reviewed. Immediate steps will be taken to ease the burden of debt and high interest rates on farm loans. Crop and livestock insurance schemes will be made more effective.

The UPA government will introduce a special programme for dryland farming in the arid and semi-arid regions of the country. Watershed and wasteland development programmes will be taken up on a massive scale. Water management in all its aspects, both for irrigation and drinking purposes, will received urgent attention.

The UPA administration will ensure the fullest implementation of minimum wage laws for farm labour. Comprehensive protective legislation will be enacted for all agricultural workers. Revenue administration will be thoroughly modernized and clear land titles will be established.

The UPA government will bring forward a Constitutional Amendment to ensure the democratic, autonomous and professional functioning of co-operatives.

Controls that depress the incomes of farmers will be systematically removed. Farmers will be given greater say in the organizations that supply inputs to them.

The UPA government will ensure that adequate protection is provided to all farmers from imports, particularly when international prices fall sharply.

The UPA government will ensure that government agencies entrusted with the responsibility for procurement and marketing will pay special attention to farmers in poor and backward states and districts. Farmers all over the country will receive fair and remunerative prices. The terms of trade will be maintained in favour of agriculture.

The UPA government will take steps to ensure that dues to all farmers including sugarcane farmers will be cleared at the earliest.

Education, Health

The UPA government pledges to raise public spending in education to least 6% of GDP with at least half this amount being spent of primary and secondary sectors. This will be done in a phased manner.

The UPA government will introduce a cess on all central taxes to finance the commitment to universalize access to quality basic education. A National Commission on Education will be set-up to allocate resources and monitor programmes.

The UPA government will take immediate steps to reverse the trend of communalization of education that had set in the past five years. It will also ensure that all institutions of higher learning and professional education retain their autonomy. The UPA will ensure that nobody is denied professional education because he or she is poor.

Academic excellence and professional competence will be the sole criteria for all appointments to bodies like the Indian Council for Historical Research, Indian Council for Social Science Research, University Grants Commission, National Council for Educational Research and Training, etc. Steps will be taken to remove the communalization of the school syllabus that has taken place in the past five years. A review committee of experts will be set-up for this purpose.

A national cooked nutritious mid-day meal scheme funded mainly by the central government, will be introduced in primary and secondary schools. An appropriate mechanism for quality checks will also set-up. The UPA will also universalize the Integrated Child Development Services (ICDS) scheme to provide a functional Anganwadi in every settlement and ensure full coverage for all children. The UPA government will fully back and support all NGO efforts in the area of primary education. Proper infrastructure will be created in schools for NCC. NSS, physical development, sports and cultural development of all students.

The UPA government will raise public spending on health to at least 2-3% of GDP over the next five years with focus on primary health care. A national scheme for health insurance for poor families will be introduced. The UPA will step up public investment in programmes to control all communicable diseases and also provide leadership to the national AIDS control effort.

The UPA government will take all steps to ensure availability of life-savings drugs at reasonable prices. Special attention will be paid to the poorer sections in the matter of health care. The feasibility of reviving public sector units set-up for the manufacture of critical bulk drugs will be re-examined so as to bring down and keep a check on prices of drugs.

Women and Children

The UPA government will take the lead to introduce legislation for one-third reservations for women in Vidhan Sabhas and in the Lok Sabha. Legislation on domestic violence and against gender discrimination will be enacted.

The UPA government will ensure that at least one-third of all funds flowing into panchayats will be earmarked for programmes for the development of women and children. Village women and their associations will be encouraged to assume responsibility for all development schemes relating to drinking water, sanitation, primary education, health and nutrition.

Complete legal equality for women in all spheres will be made a practical reality, especially by removing discriminatory legislation and by enacting new legislation that gives women, for instance, equal rights of ownership of assets like houses and land.

The UPA government will bring about a major expansion in schemes for micro-finance based on self-help groups, particularly in the backward and ecologically fragile areas of the country.

The UPA government is committed to replicating all over the country the success that some southern and other states have had in family planning. A sharply targeted population control programme will be launched in the 150-odd high-fertility districts. The UPA government recognizes that states that achieve success in family planning cannot be penalized.

The UPA government will protect the rights of children, strive for the elimination of child labour, ensure facilities for schooling and extend special care to the girl child.

Food and Nutrition Security

The UPA will work out, in the next three months, a comprehensive medium-term strategy for food and nutrition security. The objective will be to move towards universal food security over time, if found feasible.

The UPA government will strengthen the Public Distribution System (PDS) particularly in the poorest and backward blocks of the country and also involve women's and ex-servicemen's co-operatives in its management. Special schemes to reach foodgrains to the most destitute and infirm will be launched. Grain Banks in chronically food-scarce areas will be established. Antyodaya cards for all households at risk of hunger will be introduced.

The UPA government will bring about major improvements in the functioning of the Food Corporation of India (FCI) to control inefficiencies that increase the food subsidy burden.

Nutrition programmes, particularly for the girl child will be expanded on a significant scale.

Panchayati Raj

The UPA government will ensure that all funds for poverty alleviation and rural development programmes will be credited directly to panchayat bodies as per the recommendations of the Finance Commission. The terms of reference of the Finance Commission will be formulated suitably. Appropriate guidelines will be prepared in consultation with the state governments for the effective utilization of such funds.

Devolution of funds will be accompanied by similar devolution of functions and functionaries as well. Regular elections to panchayat bodies will be ensured and the amended Act is respect of the Fifth and Sixth Schedule Areas will be implemented.

The UPA government will ensure that the Gram Sabha is empowered to emerge as the foundation of Panchayati Raj.

Scheduled Castes, Scheduled Tribes

The UPA will urge the states to make legislation for conferring ownership rights in respect of minor forest produce, including tendu patta, on all those people from the weaker sections who work in the forests.

All reservation quotas, including those relating to promotions, will be fulfilled in a time-bound manner. To codify all reservations, a Reservation Act will be enacted.

The UPA government will launch a comprehensive national programme for minor irrigation of all lands owned by *dalits* and *adivasis*. Landless families will be endowed with land through implementation of land ceiling and land redistribution legislation. No reversal of ceilings legislation will be permitted.

The UPA administration will take all measures to reconcile the objectives of economic growth and environmental conservation, particularly as far as tribal communities dependent on forests are concerned.

The UPA is concerned with the growth of extremist violence and other forms of terrorist activity in different states. This is not merely a law-and-order problem, but a far deeper socio-economic issue which will be addressed more meaningfully than has been the case so far. False encounters will not be permitted.

The UPA government will immediately review the overall strategy and programmes for the development of tribal areas to plug loopholes and to work out more viable livelihood strategies. In addition, more effective systems of relief and rehabilitation will be put in place for tribal and other groups displaced by development projects. Tribal people alienated from land will be rehabilitated.

The UPA government is very sensitive to the issue of affirmative action, including reservations, in the private sector. It will immediately initiate a national dialogue with all political parties, industry and other organizations to see how best the private sector can fulfil the aspirations of scheduled caste and scheduled tribe youth.

Eviction of tribal communities and other forest-dwelling communities from forest areas will be discontinued. Cooperation of these communities will be sought for protecting forests and for undertaking social afforestation. The rights of tribal communities over mineral resources, water sources, etc. as laid down by law will be fully safeguarded.

Social Harmony, Welfare of Minorities

The UPA is committed to the implementation of the Places of Worship (Special Provisions) Act, 1992. On Ayodhya, it will await the verdict of the courts, while encouraging negotiations between parties to the dispute for an amicable settlement which must, in turn, receive legal sanction.

The UPA government will enact a model comprehensive law to deal with communal violence and encourage each state to adopt that law to generate faith and confidence in minority communities.

The UPA government will amend the Constitution to establish a Commission for Minority Educational Institutions that will provide direct affiliation for minority professional institutions to central universities.

The UPA will promote modern and technical education among all minority communities. Social and economic empowerment of minorities through more systematic attention to education and employment will be a priority concern for the UPA.

The UPA will establish a National Commission to see how best the welfare of socially and economically backward sections among religious and linguistic minorities, including reservations in education and employment, is enhanced. The Commission will be given six months to submit its report.

Adequate funds will be provided to the National Minorities Development Corporation to ensure its effective functioning. The UPA government will examine the question of providing Constitutional status to the Minorities Commission and will also strive for recognition and promotion of Urdu language under Articles 345 and 347 of the Constitution.

The National Integration Council will be restructured and revived so as to fulfil its original objectives. It will meet at least twice a year.

Infrastructure

The UPA attaches the highest priority to the development and expansion of physical infrastructure like roads, highways, ports, power, railways, water supply, sewage treatment and sanitation. Public investment in infrastructure will be enhanced, even as the role of the private sector is expanded. Subsidies will be made explicit and provided through the budget.

The review of the Electricity Act, 2003 will be undertaken in view of the concern expressed by a number of states. The mandatory date of June 10, 2004 for unbundling and replacing the state electricity boards will be extended. The UPA government also reiterates its commitment to an increased role for private generation of power and more importantly power distribution.

The UPA government commits itself to a comprehensive programme of urban renewal and to a massive expansion of social housing in towns and cities, paying particular attention to the needs of slum-dwellers. Housing for the weaker sections in rural areas will be expanded on a large scale. Forced eviction and demolition of slums will be stopped and while undertaking urban renewal, care will be taken to see that the urban and semi-urban poor are provided housing near their place of occupation.

The UPA will pay special attention to augmenting and modernizing rural infrastructure consisting of roads, irrigation, electrification, cold-chain and marketing outlets. All existing irrigation projects will be completed with three to four years. Household electrification will be completed in five years.

Water Resources

The UPA government will make a comprehensive assessment of the feasibility of linking the rivers of the country starting with the south-bound rivers. This assessment will be done in a fully consultative manner. It will also explore the feasibility of linking sub-basins of rivers in states like Bihar. The UPA will take all steps to ensure that long-pending inter-state disputes on rivers and water-sharing like the Cauvery Waters dispute are settled amicably at the earliest keeping in mind the interests of all parties to the dispute.

To put an end to the acute drinking water shortage in cities, especially in southern states, desalination plants will be installed all along the Coromandel Coast starting with Chennai. Special problems of habitations in hilly terrains will be addressed immediately.

Providing drinking water to all sections in urban and rural areas and augmenting availability of drinking water sources is an issue of the topmost priority. Harvesting rain water, desilting existing ponds and other innovative mechanisms will be adopted.

Regional Development, Centre-State Relations

The UPA government is committed to redressing growing regional imbalances both among states as well as within states, through fiscal, administrative, investment and other means. It is a matter of concern that regional imbalances have been accentuated by not just historical neglect but also by distortions in Plan allocations and central government assistance. Even in the Tenth Five Year Plan , states like Bihar, Assam and UP have received per capita allocations that are much below the national average. The UPA government will consider the creation of a Backward States Grant Fund that will be used to create productive assets in these states. The central government will also take proactive measures to speed up the industrialization of the eastern and north-eastern region.

A structured and transparent approach to alleviate the burden of debt on states will be adopted at the earliest, so as to enable them to increase social sector investments. Interest rates on loans to states will be reduced and the share of states in the single, divisible pool of taxes enhanced.

All non-statutory resource transfers from the central government will be weighted in favour of poor and backward states but with performance parameters as well. A special programme for social and physical infrastructure development in the poorest and most backward districts of the country will be taken up on a priority basis.

The UPA government will take special measures to ensure that regions of India like in the east where the credit-deposit ratio is lagging, is improved substantially.

The UPA government will review the issue of payment of royalties to states in the area of minerals.

From time to time, previous governments have announced special economic packages as, for example, for the north-east, for Bihar and for J & K. For Bihar, Shri Rajiv Gandhi had announced a special development package in 1989 and subsequently another package was announced at the time of its division in 1999 to make up for the loss of revenue. These packages will be implemented expeditiously.

The UPA government will make the National Development Council (NDC) a more effective instrument of co-operative federalism. The NDC will meet at least twice a year and in different states. Immediately, the NDC will take up the issue of the financial health of states and arrive at a national consensus on specific steps to be taken in this regard. The Inter-State Council will also be activated. All centrally-sponsored schemes except in national priority areas like family planning will be transferred to states.

The UPA government will consider the demand for the formation of a Telangana state at an appropriate time after due consultations and consensus.

The Sarkaria Commission had last looked at the issue of Centre-State relations over two decades ago. The UPA government will set-up a new Commission for this purpose keeping in view the sea-changes that have taken place in the polity and economy of India since then.

Long-pending schemes in specific states that have national significance, like the Sethu Samuthuiram Project, flood control and drainage in North Bihar (that requires co-operation with Nepal as well) and Prevention of Erosion in Padma-Ganga and Bhagirathi flood control in West Bengal will be completed expeditiously. A Flood-prone Area Development Programme will be started and the central government will fully support flood control works in inter-state and international rivers. All existing schemes for drought-prone area development will be reviewed and a single major national programme launched.

Jammu and Kashmir, North-East

The UPA government is pledged to respecting the letter and spirit of Article 370 of the Constitution that accords a special status to J & K. Dialogue with all groups and with different shades of opinion in J & K will be pursued on a sustained basis, in consultation with the democratically-elected state government. The healing touch policy pursued by the state government will be fully supported and an economic and humanitarian thrust provided to it. The state will be given every assistance to rebuild its infrastructure quickly. New efforts will be launched to bring investments in areas like power, tourism, handicrafts and sericulture.

The UPA government is determined to tackle terrorism, militancy and insurgency in the north-east as a matter of urgent national priority. All north-eastern states will be given special assistance to upgrade and expand infrastructure. The North-eastern Council will be strengthened and given adequate professional support. The territorial integrity of existing states will be maintained.

Administrative Reforms

The UPA will set-up an Administrative Reforms Commission to prepare a detailed blueprint for revamping the public administration system. E-governance will be promoted on a massive scale. The Right to Information Act will be made more progressive, participatory and meaningful. The Lok Pal Bill will be enacted into law.

The UPA government will take the leadership role to drastically cut delays in High Courts and lower levels of the judiciary. Legal aid services will be expanded. Judicial reforms will be given a fresh momentum.

As part of its commitment to electoral reforms, the UPA will initiate steps to introduce state funding of elections at the earliest.

Industry

The UPA will take all necessary steps to revive industrial growth and put it on a robust footing, through a range of policies including deregulation, where necessary incentives to boost private investment will be introduced. FDI will continue to be encouraged and actively sought particularly in areas of infrastructure, high-technology and exports and where local assets and employment are created on a significant scale. The country needs and can easily absorb at least two to three times the present level of FDI inflows. Indian industry will be given every support to become productive and competitive. All regulatory institutions will be strengthened to ensure that competition is free and fair. These institutions will be run professionally.

The UPA government will set-up a National Manufacturing Competitiveness Council to provide a continuing forum for policy dialogue to energise and sustain the growth of manufacturing industry like food processing, textiles and garments, engineering, consumer goods, pharmaceuticals, capital goods, leather, and IT hardware.

Household and artisanal manufacturing will be given greater technological, investment and marketing support. In the past few years, the most employment-intensive segment of Small-Scale Industry (SSI) has suffered extensively. A major promotional package for the SSI sector will be announced soon. It will be freed from the Inspector Raj and given full credit, technological and marketing support. Infrastructure upgradation in major industrial clusters will receive urgent attention.

Competition in the financial sector will be expanded. Public sector banks will be given full managerial autonomy. Interest rates will provide incentives both to investors and savers, particularly pensioners and senior citizens. The UPA government will never take decisions on the Employers Provident Fund (EPF) without consultations with and approval of the EPF Board. Regulation of urban co-operative banks in particular and of banks in general will be made more effective. LIC and GIC will continue to be in the public sector and will continue to play their social role. In addition, the social obligations imposed by regulatory bodies on private banks and private insurance companies will be monitored and enforced strictly.

Labour

The UPA government is firmly committed to ensure the welfare and well-being of all workers, particularly those in the unorganized sector who constitute 93% of our workforce. Social security, health insurance and other schemes for such workers like weavers, handloom workers, fishermen and fisherwomen, toddy tappers, leather workers, plantation labour, beedi workers, etc. will be expanded.

The UPA rejects the idea of automatic hire and fire. It recognizes that some changes in labour laws may be required but such changes must fully protect the interests of workers and families and must take place after full consultation with trade unions. The UPA will pursue a dialogue with industry and trade unions on this issue before coming up with specific proposals. However, labour laws other than the Industrial Disputes Act that create an Inspector Raj will be re-examined and procedures harmonized and streamlined.

The UPA government firmly believes that labour-management relations in our country must be marked by consultations, co-operation and consensus, not confrontation. Tripartite consultations with trade unions and industry on all proposals concerning them will be actively pursued. Rights and benefits earned by workers, including the right to strike according to law, will not be taken away or curtailed.

Public Sector

The UPA government is committed to a strong and effective public sector whose social objectives are met by its commercial functioning. But for this, there is need for selectivity and a strategic focus. The UPA is pledged to devolve full managerial and commercial autonomy to successful, profit-making companies operating in a competitive environment. Generally profit-making companies will not be privatized.

All privatizations will be considered on a transparent and consultative case-by-case basis. The UPA will retain existing "navaratna" companies in the public sector while these companies raise resources from the capital market. While every effort will be made to modernize and restructure sick public sector companies and revive sick industry, chronically loss-making companies will either be sold-off, or closed, after all workers have got their legitimate dues and compensation. The UPA will induct private industry to turn-around companies that have potential for revival.

The UPA government believes that privatization should increase competition, not decrease it. It will not support the emergence of any monopoly that only restrict competition. It also believes that there must be a direct link between privatization and social needs—like, for example, the use of privatization revenues for designated social sector schemes. Public sector companies and nationalized banks will be encouraged to enter the capital market to raise resources and offer new investment avenues to retail investors.

Fiscal Policy

The UPA government commits itself to eliminating the revenue deficit of the centre by 2009, so as to release more resources for investments in social and physical infrastructure. All subsidies will be targeted sharply at the poor and the truly needy like small and marginal farmers, farm labour and the urban poor. A detailed roadmap for accomplishing this will be unveiled in Parliament within 90 days. The UPA government will not cut deficits by reducing or curtailing growth of investment and development outlays.

The UPA government is pledged to the early introduction of VAT after all the necessary technical and administrative homework has been completed, particularly on issues like the integration of service sector taxation and compensation to states. It will initiate measures to increase the tax: GDP ratio by undertaking major tax reforms that expand the base of tax-payers, increase tax compliance and make the tax administration more efficient. Tax rates will be stable and conducive to growth, compliance and investment. Special schemes to unearth black money and assets will be introduced.

The UPA government will take effective and strong measures to control the price hike of essential commodities. Provisions to deal with speculators, hoarders and black-marketeers under the Essential Commodities Act will not be diluted in any way.

Capital Markets

The UPA government is deeply committed, through tax and other policies, to the orderly development and functioning of capital markets that reflect the true fundamentals of the economy. Financial markets will be deepened. FIIs will continue to be encouraged while the vulnerability of the financial system to the flow of speculative capital will be reduced. Misuse of double taxation agreements will be stopped. Interests of small investors will be protected and they will be given new avenues for safe investment of their savings. SEBI will be further strengthened. Strictest action will be taken against market manipulators and those who try to deliberately engineer market panic.

Economic Reforms

The UPA reiterates its abiding commitment to economic reforms with a human face, that stimulates growth, investment and employment. Further reforms are needed and will be carried out in agriculture, industry and services. The UPA's economic reforms will be oriented primarily to spreading and deepening rural prosperity, to significantly improving the quality of public systems and delivery of public services, to bringing about a visible and tangible difference in the quality of life of ordinary citizens of our country.

Defence, Internal Security

The UPA government will ensure that all delays in the modernization of the armed forces are eliminated and that all funds earmarked for modernization are spent fully at the earliest.

The UPA will set-up a new Department of Ex-Servicemens' Welfare in the Ministry of Defence. The long pending issue of one-rank, one-pension will be re-examined.

The UPA government will make the National Security Council a professional and effective institution.

The UPA government is committed to maintaining a credible nuclear weapons programme while at the same time it will evolve demonstrable and verifiable confidence-building measures with its nuclear neighbours. It will take a leadership role in promoting universal, nuclear disarmament and working for a nuclear weapons-free world.

The UPA has been concerned with the manner in which POTA has been grossly misused in the past two years. There will be no compromise in the fight against terrorism. But given the abuse of POTA that has taken place, the UPA government will repeal it, while existing laws are enforced strictly.

The UPA government will take the strictest possible action, without fear or favour, against all those individuals and organizations who spread social discord, disturb social amity, propagate religious bigotry and communal hatred. The law of the land will be enforced effectively.

Science and Technology

The UPA government will follow policies and introduce programmes that strengthen India's vast science and technology infrastructure. Science and technology development and application missions will be launched in key areas, covering both global leadership and local transformation. The UPA government will mobilize the skills and expertise of Indian scientists, technologists and other professionals working abroad for institution-building and other projects in the country.

Energy Security

The UPA government will immediately put in place policies to enhance the country's energy security particularly in the area of oil. Overseas investments in the hydrocarbon industry will be actively encouraged. An integrated energy policy linked with sustainable development will be put in place.

Foreign Policy, International Organisations

The UPA government will pursue an independent foreign policy keeping in mind its past traditions. This policy will seek to promote multi-polarity in world relations and oppose all attempts at unilateralism.

The UPA government will give the highest priority to building closer political, economic and other ties with its neighbours in South Asia and to strengthening SAARC. Particular attention will be paid to regional projects in the area of water resources, power and ecological conservation. Dialogue with Pakistan on all issues will be pursued systematically and on a sustained basis. The UPA will support peace talks in Sri Lanka that fulfil the legitimate aspirations of Tamils and religious minorities within the territorial integrity and solidarity of Sri Lanka. Outstanding issues with Bangladesh will be resolved.

Trade and investment with China will be expanded further and talks on the border issue pursued seriously. Relationships with East Asian countries will be intensified. Traditional ties with West Asia will be given a fresh thrust. The UPA government reiterates India's decades-old commitment to the cause of the Palestinian people for a homeland of their own. Steps will be taken to withdraw Indian mercenaries from Iraq while further recruitment for this purpose will be banned.

Even as it pursues closer engagement and relations with the USA, the UPA government will maintain the independence of India's foreign policy position on all regional and global issues. The UPA is committed to deepening ties with Russia and Europe as well.

In keeping with the stance adopted by the late Shri Murasoli Maran at Doha, the UPA government will fully protect the national interest, particularly of farmers, in all WTO negotiations. Commitments made earlier will be adhered to, even as efforts are mounted to ensure that all agreements reflect our concerns fully particularly in the area of intellectual property and agriculture. The UPA government will use the flexibility afforded in existing WTO agreements to fully protect Indian agriculture and industry. The UPA government will play a proactive role in strengthening the emerging solidarity of developing countries in the shape of G-20 in the WTO.

Official Language

The UPA government will set-up a committee to examine the question of declaring all languages in the Eighth Schedule of the Constitution as official languages. In addition, Tamil will be declared as a classical language.

A Final Word

This is a common minimum programme (CMP) for the UPA government. It is, by no means, a comprehensive agenda. It is a starting point that highlights the main priorities, policies and programmes. The UPA is committed to the implementation of the CMP. This CMP is the foundation for another CMP—collective maximum performance.

8

Analysis of CMP Related Areas

In this chapter there are 29 writings by the author touching on key areas dealt under CMP of the Congress-led government. These writings would also be found useful in policy formulation of the present government in areas of rural development, agriculture, food-storage facilities, crop diversification, agri-industries, education, tribal problems and other like issues. Also there are writings that deal with corruption which has taken deep roots in the economy and is one of the major problems hindering the growth of this country and rural economy in particular.

In Section 1 there are four writings dealing with 'Small Farmers'.
In Section 2 there are two writings dealing with 'Food Pricing'.
In Section 3 there are again two writings dealing with 'Post-Green Revolution Problems'.
In the next Section 4 again there are two writings of 'Food Storage'.
In Section 5 there are five writings dealing with 'Food Surplus and Diversification'.

In Section 6 there are two writings pertaining to 'Rural Development and Panchayats'.

In Section 7 there are also two writings pertaining to 'Khadi'.

In Section 8 there are five writings pertaining to 'Corruption'.

In the last Section 9 there are four writings pertaining to 'Education'.

Section 1

SMALL FARMERS

1. Rural Development and the Poor

While the poor in rural areas need attention from their political bosses whom they have elected, the irony is that once elected these people fail to show their faces and thus the poor are left to their fate with little change occurring in their surroundings. Even it is found that while several schemes of the so-called pro-poor are in operation under the Centre's direction, these also fail to benefit the rural population for whom they are meant, as much of the resources thus available fail to reach them. It is therefore suggested that this state of fund distribution should be drastically changed in as much as that Panchayats should be made responsible for the rural development programmes and the resources for these should be routed directly to them.

Every political party makes commitments about rural development but these are invariably forgotten once it assumes power. It could be that the comfort of richly furnished bungalows and posh offices distance the people who govern from the poor *kisans* labouring in their tiny farms.

Hardly any Central or State minister takes the trouble to visit the rural areas of their constituencies. The rural populace thus continues to be deprived of basic facilities like drinking water, electricity, healthcare, education and housing. The *panchayats* were supposed to shape rural destinies with liberal help from the Centre and other agencies. But this dream has been largely unrealized.

In fact, several panchayats are yet to function properly. Those which exist often face severe funds crunch and most of what little money reaches them is siphoned-off by members who wield influence. Only a few prominent panchayats manage to draw the attention of politicians and that too for their personal interests.

On their part, *kisans* often wonder why leaders visit them frequently before the elections to assure them prosperity if they are voted to power. Yet when a farmer tries to visit his leaders, he is not even allowed into their offices by peons and bodyguards.

Multiply and Divide

Meanwhile, the single ministry of agriculture at the Centre has multiplied into a plethora of subordinate ministries. One wonders whether this has translated into any effective gain at the grass-roots level. For the ordinary villager still remains completely confused when he has to seek the help of the government. He rarely ventures into the citadels of power where he knows he will not be entertained. Therefore, it is questionable as to who benefits from these ministries which claim a giant share of the Central exchequer by way of salary and perquisites. Quite obviously, these have been created to accommodate the growing political partnerships of the government with scarcely any regard for the cumulative cost of doing so.

While several schemes of rural development have been put into operation after the haphazard expansion of the ministry of agriculture, the reality is that hardly a small percentage of the money disbursed for these have reached the target groups.

Consolidate First

Former Prime Minister, Rajiv Gandhi, in his characteristic way, had once remarked that only 10 per cent of the funds actually reach the rural areas while most of the rest get lost in the long channel of distribution. On an average, 40 per cent of the funds released by the government goes to the distributing agency, 10 per cent is spent in filling the pockets of those distantly connected with project and only around 50 per cent reach the people.

Such a situation calls for some soul-searching. The moot question is, can the situation be improved? Can we not think of better alternatives to reach out to the target groups and eliminate the middlemen? Perhaps the government should be more serious about curbing its expansion-spree. Stringent government action is required against bureaucrats and government officials who embezzle funds. For the fear of losing whatever financial help they get from governments, non-governmental organizations often fail to report against corrupt officers. Non-governmental organizations should be more forthcoming in reporting corruption.

The best solution lies in strengthening the Panchayati Raj institutions which should be made solely responsible for programmes of rural development and for which they should be provided with adequate funds. Also, panchayats should be encouraged to employ experienced people to audit their accounts. Panchayat members, drawn from the rural community itself, should be trained in efficient management. Instead of expanding the ministry of agriculture, the government should thus pay more attention to consolidating the panchayat system.

2. Small Farms are not Viable

In almost all cases the farm size has been becoming smaller with partitions of family property. Here of course small farmers have been the worst sufferers. Their holdings are no longer viable for cultivation. Consequently many of them, particularly in agriculturally prosperous state of Punjab, have leased them to bigger farmers thus helping them to widen the net of their income and fortunes of small farmers who are the actual owners have been reduced to a state of penury and several of them have virtually become landless labourers working on these farms in such capacity.

About one-third of the Indian population, that is about half of rural India, works a small or marginal farmers. Yet, there are hardly any sustainable income-yielding programmes for this section. Naturally, an overwhelming majority of these people live below the poverty line and most of the offers somehow make both ends meet.

The graveness of the problem becomes clearer on an analysis of regions such as Punjab, which have experienced the green revolution and are now agriculturally prosperous enough to fill the godowns of the Food Corporation of India. Ironically, the number of small and marginal farmers have been growing in this region. An increasing rural population has led to the fragmentation of already small land-holdings. Most of these will eventually become economically unviable.

Holding on

Many of these small farmers have leased out land to medium or large farmers on long-term contracts which, however, fetch a paltry lease rent. Some have sold their land and switched to other low-income yielding vocations. Many have migrated to other places within the country. There is very little this group can do to improve their living conditions.

If the situation is bad in Punjab, it is worse in the rest of the country. Land-holdings everywhere are being cut up into fragments. One way out is to find alternative means of employment for those members of the family who might choose go to work in the fields or who cannot be accommodated there. Thus, there would be less people to work on the same pieces of land, thus facilitating higher incomes. Another way is to encourage co-operative farming where several small pieces of land can be ploughed together as one large piece. But this system has its own drawback—clash of interest among people who join the venture. If like-minded farmer with the same level of income could be brought together, this system would perhaps have worked.

Processing Change

There is a need for a radical change in the existing cropping pattern and substituting it with other, more income-yielding ones. The present system of "limited farm cycle", confined mainly to the production of wheat and paddy, despite being the building block of the green revolution, has proved harmful to the ecology and has brought about other adverse consequences like water-logging.

Agro-processing is another area that should be looked into. One of the major reasons behind and slow growth in this sector is the lack of enthusiasm on the part of the government as also the private sector. Huge amounts of fruit, vegetables and other agricultural produce are wasted every year because we do not yet know how to utilize the media and other agencies to promote the sale of agro-products. If a rigorous programme of preserving these products and encouraging their sale is undertaken, both the farming sector and those dependent on it will be benefited.

3. Post-harvest Problems and Small Farmers

It is unfortunate that while post-harvest is the best time to earn good income small farmers fail to take advantage of such positive situation due to several constraints, which are discussed in this writing.

While post-harvest is a unique period for earning income, almost the sole income in the case of small farmers and major income for large and medium farmers, it unfortunately has a very skewed distribution more biased in favour of larger farmers and less in the case of small farmers. In fact while small farmers look to this period with a high expectation to realise good income for their hard labour during the previous months they are generally disappointed with the results. They usually end up with disproportionate earnings to their labour which are far insufficient to meet the needs of their growing families. A recent study made by experts at PAU has estimated that the average income earned by a small farmer does not exceed the salary received by a newly recruited clerk in a government department. This shows the harsh realities of the situation.

With growing families the area of an average holding has been gradually coming down. Thus, with successive partitions the average size of a farm has become quite small which is uneconomic for cultivation, little of talk to suitable mechanisation. No surprise, the average yield in Punjab, a state though blessed with the Green Revolution, has been declining, especially so in the case of small farms.

What makes these small farmers not to take full advantage of encouraging market situation of food-grains with rising prices, particularly so in the case of wheat and rice—the two staple crops in the basket of an average farmer? For this we have to look into the current credit, marketing and storage situation in particular. It is not that both Punjab and Haryana lack in modern storage, marketing as well as credit facilities. In fact, they have these in abundance compared to any other state. The basic problem is the average farmer's capacity as well as approach to make full use of these facilities.

It is well known that driven by compulsions most of the small farmers borrow heavily mainly from the *arhtias* (middlemen) with whom they have close links and when unable to repay these borrowings they are invariably driven to sell their produce to them at prices lower than those fixed by the government. Thus, their produce hardly reaches organised *mandis*.

How are then modern *mandis* with all facilities of much help to them? *Arhtias* not only take their produce in lieu of past debt but they also advance them further credit to meet their seasonal needs. Thus, a sort of vicious circle is created from where the small farmer finds it difficult to come out.

Even when he has surplus produce he finds it difficult to store it for better days when the prices are higher. Here he faces poor storage facilities in areas around. Even where rural godowns have been created a study made a few years ago had revealed gross inadequacies of these facilities where it was found that hardly any safety existed to protect the stored grain. Farmers, thus, hesitated to use these godowns which lay mostly in a deserted state.

Of course, we do have modern storage facilities but then these are beyond the reach of the small farmer, though these come to easy rescue of big and medium farmers who are able to sell their produce at higher prices later.

We do talk of diversification of agriculture in the interest of small farmers for earning higher income and advise them to take to alternative more value adding and income-yielding activities like vegetables, dairy, poultry, even horticulture and floriculture where there is rising demand. But then the poor and illiterate farmer, who is financially and technically ill-equipped, is in a state of confusion. He badly needs proper guidance, financial support and technical assistance where we talk much but do little.

The result is that he is back to square one from where he finds no escape. It is a big struggle for him and we must come out with practical approach and avoid sermonising.

Incidentally most of the problems faced by these farmers in the post-harvest period are also due to their lack of education where the high average income states of Punjab and Haryana are badly let down. Hardly there is need to repeat that we must learn from the experience of Kerala which has demonstrated that successful universal education wipes out ignorance and helps in creating an egalitarian society.

4. Some Lessons from History

Most of the developed countries have reduced the size of agriculture labour by developing alternative sectors like industry and infrastructure. A close study of India would show that here the farm population instead of declining after green revolution, has actually risen further, thereby indicating that at present a far larger workforce depends on agriculture as principal means of sustenance compared to the past.

The experience of present developed countries shows that their initial development process too had been through the route of agriculture, where a large number of their population had been employed. In due course, however, there was a quantum shift of this manpower to alternative sectors, especially industry and infrastructure. And today most of these countries just have around 10 per cent of their working population in agriculture, while a very large percentage has shifted to secondary and tertiary sectors. Even with small percentage of population in the farm sector it is found that they are able to produce far larger quantity of food than earlier.

This remarkable inter-sectoral shift has been the result of fast mechanisation of farm sector and the introduction of better inputs, storage and marketing facilities and improvement in communications.

With this happening, a pertinent question arises, why this type of transformation has failed to happen in India where some north-western states have by now witnessed a sustained growth in agriculture over the last four decades? In fact, a close study would show that here the farm population instead of declining after green revolution, has actually risen further, thereby indicating that at present a far larger workforce depends on agriculture as principal means of sustenance compared to earlier. Such sustained pressure of population has further lowered the average farm size where in today's land scenario it is by and large dominated by a new class of small and marginal farmers who under the changed conditions find it difficult to survive.

Studies have confirmed that average income derived from by a small farmer in Punjab is not equivalent to the salary of a fresh recruit in the government service at the bottom who, of course, is not to labour so hard or is loaded so much with family responsibility as is a small marginal farmer.

Little surprise that several of these farmers have turned into agricultural labourers or shifted to other areas to supplement their income.

The question still persists. Why this has happened? Why this experience has gone counter to what we have witnessed in the case of present developed economies who were able to shift a large proportion of their population from agriculture to alternative areas and which in itself with growing shortage of farm hands had helped fast mechanisation of the farm sector?

What is wrong with our economies—like Punjab, Haryana and other states which have spearheaded green revolution, that they should have failed to follow the same course as history dictates? First of all, India being a confederation of several states where farm revolution is confined to only a few states, is in itself not a valid premise for this sort of comparison for simple reason that it has yet not touched the national frontier and the time horizon is too small. Besides, India has been able to achieve such quick growth basically because of easy access to new farm technology and inputs which had not developed still when advanced nations were transforming their agriculture. They took much longer to accomplish this task. Thus, they could have a stable foundation unlike India.

Secondly, conditions were different when the present developed economies were growing. They had smaller population—some had very small—and they had also comparatively larger agricultural area.

In fact, in case of North America land was so abundant that taming it in itself was a major problem compared to their smaller population. For them land has never been a problem. Even when quite a few European countries faced the land problem in the 19th century, it was easier for their large population to migrate to empty areas in North America, even Australia and other countries and those who stayed back had comfortable man-land ratio. Our country, on the other hand, is faced with a different situation. Here agrarian land is limited and in the absence of opportunities for global or even internal migration, the pressure has been building up on this limited land area, which in itself has gone against modernisation of agriculture. Even in case of states which have witnessed green revolution the situation is now gradually becoming grim with fast declining man-land ratio.

Third, states like Punjab and Haryana which have been longest in the green revolution scenario constitute only small area of this sub-continent and they could, thus by no stretch of imagination bring about a radical change in their non-farm areas when at the same time they lack in natural resources needed to help to build a strong and solid base of modern industries. And they face acute power problem, while power is so essential for the growth of modern industries.

Fourth, one has also to discount the factor like long period of instability and terrorism that Punjab in particular, had to face with two major wars fought with Pakistan and long era of insurgency which completely ruined even what little industrial potential it had created.

Fifth, the government policies of populism in the shape of providing free power and irrigation mostly on political considerations have also stood in the way of industrialisation in as much as that a part of loss thus sustained is recovered through charging higher tariff on power supplied to industry and also the supply is often erratic. Even the basic facilities for industrial growth are also missing and it appears that the government has hardly put its mind on improving them. Infact, it has treated industry as a low priority area, by giving its attention to agriculture.

Under these circumstances industry has failed to make any headway, though in the larger interest the growth should have been industry-intensive which alone would have helped to take away much of the burden from the ailing farm sector.

In fact, during their growth the present advanced economies had accorded a high priority to industrialisation and basic services. Look at the history of Western Europe where industrial revolution came much earlier than in other countries. Such industrialisation had helped enormously these countries to absorb excess manpower from the crowded farms.

Similarly, the history of Japan also tells us how the development of its industry through state intervention and patronage had been able to absorb excess load of manpower from the farm sector. Little surprise that with just 15 per cent of land available for cultivation Japan did not face any crowding in agriculture. Thus, some lessons should be drawn from the experience of advanced economies as well as some developing economies (China in particular) which shows that, while agriculture is very important for meeting the basic need of food it at the same time calls for parallel attention to the development of industry and infrastructure. In fact, while such growth helps to absorb excess manpower from agriculture it also helps further growth of farm sector itself.

Today's problem of plenty of food stocks would not have been there had we gone in for the creation of non-farm opportunities on large scale, which would have injected sufficient income particularly with people below the poverty line who would have thus been in a position to buy these stocks of grain.

Section 2

FOOD PRICING

5. Politics of Food Pricing

There has been a bungling over the current paddy pricing issue as both the Congress government and the opposition SAD-BJP combine in Punjab have been playing dirty politics to gain mileage.

In the recent history the paddy crop this season has been least among all the three paddy surplus states of Punjab,

Haryana and Andhra Pradesh. With the monsoon failing to save the scorching fields which destroyed a good part of the paddy crop and floods in the month of September (at least in Punjab and Haryana) further added to the woes of farmers. Arrival of paddy this season to various *mandis* had been down to trickle compared to the situation earlier. But it has even failed to alleviate the suffering of farmers who looked for higher prices to compensate for the loss suffered by them.

Normally a failed major food crop would help in raising its market price to a sufficient level to compensate farmers. But this time unlike the past it did not make any difference—rather distress sales of paddy have been reported when the farmers had to empty their stocks in the godowns of *Arhtiyas* (middleman) to obtain timely monetary relief when the prices realised have been much lower than fixed under minimum support price (MSP) last year when there was far better harvest. Further, there has been delay in the announcement of MSP for the current year while last year this announcement was made not only much earlier but even the government's operations for the purchase of paddy had started in the month of April simultaneously along with the arrival of paddy.

Thus, farmers had to face double shock, one, delayed announcement of MSP, second, the Centre's total failure to compensate them for the loss suffered due to failure of harvest when they expected a price of around Rs. 750 per quintal. But the government has stuck to last year's price of Rs. 530 which has been hailed as a cruel joke by the farmers who have totally rejected it and have in consequence taken to the street. A large number of them had camped in Chandigarh to make themselves heard by the seat of power.

There is a strong feeling that there has been high political bungling in the current paddy issue as both the ruling Congress government and the opposition SAD-BJP combine in Punjab have been playing dirty politics to gain political mileage out of the paddy crisis. While the chief minister Amarinder Singh held a *dharna* outside the residence of Prime Minister along with his party members and courted arrest, opposition leaders have preferred to stay away from such tactics. On the other hand, Akali Dal leader Badal had personally met the Prime Minister along with other supporters to drive home the plight of farmers and the need for more liberal support price. As a result, the government has made marginal addition of Rs. 20 to the MSP announced—this adjustment incidentally comes closer to the average raise of MSP during the last 10 years.

It has also been agreed to consider suitable bonus to the aggrieved farmers. Now the Congress has not agreed to the MSP announced which they demand at Rs. 666 for common paddy and Rs. 726 for Grade A paddy, besides Rs. 100 minimum bonus per quintal above MSP. It is most unlikely to be agreed upon by the Centre. Akalis have maintained silence over it and are relying more on liberal bonus as a special case this fiscal year due to unwarranted whether situation causing high damage to paddy crop.

It is well-known that the current distressing paddy situation has been used as a peg to hang the Centre's stick to beat the Congress government and BJP is trying to boost the image of its earlier partner SAD.

Congress leaders have openly criticised the Centre's partisan attitude.

However, the Centre's version is quite different. They claim that there has been no consensus on the part of the state government and the opposition parties on this issue. The MSP demand from the ruling party was voiced quite late and then it did not bear any accordance to the reality of circumstances when the Centre was already loaded with excess stocks of food-grains and could not afford to pay a high price.

Further by agreeing to high uneconomic price the message would have gone to the farmers that they could continue to produce as much paddy they chose next year, when in fact everybody agreed that time has come to adopt harsh measures to reduce its production. And here lower MSP was the only major step to force them to agree. The government in fact has been liberal in MSP in case of oilseeds as it wants farmers to divert to its production and come out of paddy crop.

The stand-off between the Centre and Punjab continues on this paddy issue. But on the whole, the message which has gone home to the farmers is that under the prevailing circumstances the Congress government could hardly take any concrete measures to help them. Although they do not have faith in Akalis, farmers still feel that Akali leaders could help in getting concessions like higher subsidy on inputs as well as more helpful attitude towards irrigation and power supply.

While Punjab may have been let down by the Centre because of it being a Congress ruled state, then what about other two paddy surplus states of Haryana and Andhra Pradesh which too have suffered under the current situation of drought?

But these states are not that important in surplus paddy generation as is Punjab. Normally, the lead for paddy MSP generally comes from Punjab which has turned record producer of paddy recently. Further in case of Haryana it is the production of *basmati* which is not much affected in the current situation.

It also appears the governments of A.P. and Haryana did not push forward the MSP issue as they wanted to side with SAD leadership. This becomes evident when they had joined hands with Badal in a special meeting with the Prime Minister and successfully pressed forward the issue of reconsideration of MSP in paddy keeping the larger interest of farmers in view.

This time the question of MSP for paddy assumed more than the usual political overtone mainly because the principal surplus paddy producing state of Punjab is controlled by the Congress. Had it been controlled by the SAD-BJP combine the issue along with the amount of MSP and bonus would have been favourably tackled.

The image of Congress has been tarnished due to this in Punjab. Added to it farmers were already displeased by its anti-Kisan stand like stopping of free power and water supply, particularly at a time when the state had faced crisis situation in paddy cultivation.

The present Congress government has also failed to tackle the issue faced by farmers to move away from paddy cultivation. This is having its adverse impact on environment particularly in rural areas and has thus brought misery to the local population. It is as well becoming non-productive as rising output cost of paddy is proving difficult to sell it at a remunerative price.

The government should first set its own house in order before expecting farmers to follow the course of farm diversification as suggested by them. Both the Centre and states would have to work in tandem for evolving a suitable strategy.

Thus instead of politicising the MSP issue the Punjab government should get down to achieve the task of diversifying farm production on a scientific and acceptable way. Even the agricultural universities in the country can be actively involved to work out a new strategy.

6. Need for Transparency

Though government has announced the reduction in food prices for three months, it is the purchasing capacity of people which has to be improved. More purchasing capacity can only be created through opening of large scale employment avenues for rural mass. We need not sell our food abroad at near distress prices, when right in our country we have a big market to feed the semi-starved population.

Currently our country has accumulated 64 million tonnes of food stocks (both wheat and rice) in its godowns. Soon with the completion of wheat operations in Punjab, Haryana and other states more million tonnes of food-grains are expected to flood the *mandis* thus creating more difficult stock situation. It may be added that the creation and maintenance of capacity beyond the needed level is highly resource as well as space consuming.

It is in this context that the latest move of the government to reduce temporarily for three months the issue price of food-grains by Rs. 100 per quintal for the families above the poverty line under public distribution system is to be welcomed. Through such system it is expected to help off-take of both wheat and rice when the quantity available per family would be 35 kg per month. It is uniform for all category of consumers irrespective of their poverty line and also for those who are covered under Antyodaya scheme. Further, there has been no change in the prices of food supplied to the families falling below the poverty line (including Antyodaya) where the prices per kg. of wheat and rice (Rs. 4.15 and Rs. 5.65 respectively) are already lower compared to revised prices of above grains (Rs. 5.10 and Rs. 7.30 respectively).

The Centre has also announced to boost the export of food-grains stating that the export prices would not be below the prices charge by BPL households, which is claimed to be lower than international prices. There are certain loopholes in the announced system. First of all, the system is valid for only three months and the reason is not explained. Possibly, it is just to know the response from families covered under PDS.

Second, since the price of wheat and rice supplied to families below the poverty line (including Antyodaya members) has not been revised one can safely conclude that the situation is not going to show any change in demand from these families.

However, how far they would respond to the increase in family quota would again depends on the buying capacity of the families.

In fact, it is the APL families using the route of PDS are expected to respond favourably to the lowering price. But the system being open for three months alone they could enjoy the offer depending on extra income. There is a chance of private sector challenging the government effort by offering food-grains of better quality on equally competitive prices, which is likely to happen after the arrival of fresh stocks. Consumers would be tempted to buy better quality and fresh food even it is costs a little higher than the subsidised prices.

Thus, it may not be appropriate time for the government to release its stock at lower price. It may not help even to woo its own customers much less to create new ones which it is contemplating through release of five million tonnes of wheat and one million tonnes of rice in the open market at a price yet to be determined.

The price would be higher than the price announced under public distribution system. But if it is too high than it would not work when consumers have access to private stocks with facilities not available under the government system.

So far as the possibility of creating export market is concerned, even with prices equivalent to highly subsidised sale to consumers below the poverty line, it appears that the global market, which is quality conscious, is not going to hold out much promise.

To overcome this problem India has to tag the domestic market where still a large number of people are unable to afford even highly subsidised food due to lack of purchasing capacity. Thus, the basic problem is how to create purchasing capacity.

Obviously more purchasing capacity can only be created through opening of large scale employment avenues for lower jobs—the so-called labour-intensive jobs which do not require skills. It is this manpower, which is illiterate and unskilled, that has totally failed to benefit from globalisation.

We have virtually ended up in a jobless economy and even jobs created for talented professionals have been illusory and many unemployment people are waiting for their turn.

We have even failed to provide any worthwhile help to the rural population, which is burgeoning and most of the rural people are unemployed.

We need not sell our food abroad at near distress prices, when right in our country we have a big market to feed the semi-starved population by providing them with minimum employment avenues.

Let us concentrate more on rural job creating progamme in areas like rural communication, housing, electrification, water supply and other areas of capital formation, rather than on globalisation.

SECTION 3

POST-GREEN REVOLUTION PROBLEMS

7. After Green Revolution, Threat to Ecology

The problem of large scale cultivation of paddy which has led to high social fallout in rural areas and disturbed the ecology of this area, should be tackled with great care through concerted efforts on several fronts to encourage the most feasible and environment friendly land-use.

It is indeed remarkable that from a high deficit state after independence Punjab had during the next two decades moved on to the highway of green revolution and soon it was contributing substantially to the country's foodgrain kitty to feed its bulging population. There was virtual revolution in grain production and Punjab produced bumper harvest of wheat year after year which provided high surplus to meet the needs of deficit states. Not only this. Soon the country which had been importing wheat from the US and there were regular shipments of heavy imports imposing high burden on the country's weak economy, had stopped by the early seventies and the country was soon on the road to self-sufficiency in wheat production.

Apart from saving our scarce resources being diverted to food imports, it brought about food security in the country and an encouraging rise in the income of farmers both in Punjab and Haryana, as the latter also rose equally to the occasion soon after its creation round about this time.

Such grain revolution could not have been possible without access to high yielding variety of seeds as well as the needed infrastructure where irrigation facilities, fertilisers, new farm machinery, good rural roads, power supply and marketing facilities are essential ingredients. Punjab was again the first state in the country to realise the importance of these facilities and its government devoted special efforts in their creation. Liberal loans were also provided to farmers to have access to these facilities, particularly to buy costly farm machinery and improve their irrigation facilities where gradually tubewells replaced dependence on rainfall and other undependable means like canals and wells.

Realising the importance of rural power supply the government went ahead in creating such facility in rural areas which facilitated the operation of tubewells at cheaper rates for power was highly subsidised and agriculture also got priority in its supply over the needs of industry and other sectors. This helped in fast spread of tubewells and other farm machinery and Punjab today occupies the highest position in the country in tubewells, tractors and other farm machinery. This state also occupies top slot in the consumption of fertilisers, insecticides and other important inputs for sustaining green revolution.

It has also the largest network of *Mandis* in the country where several of them are equipped with the latest facilities for handling market arrivals within the minimum time. These *Mandis* are also within the easy reach of farmers and they have no longer to travel long distance to sell their produce. Alongside liberal storage facilities are also available both in rural areas and towns by the state agencies as well as FCI which helps in safe storage of food-grains.

Thus, noteworthy achievements have been made by the state government within a short time bringing it to the top position not only in food production, but equally in per capita income which is the highest in the country and even nearly double compared to backward states. In this respect Haryana also closely follows which has also witnessed a big rise in its food economy.

After the creation of abundant irrigation and power facilities, farmers had begun to cultivate paddy in a big way which soon became the second important crop after wheat. Thus soon virtually 2-crop model, wheat in winter and rice in summer, became the production model with an average farmer. And with such combination the average farmer's income made a quantum jump encouraging them for further modernisation of the farm sector, more of the latest machinery, further rise on the use of fertilisers and insecticides to give quick boost to their crops.

Thus allured to maximise his income within short time he has been working on the farm year around without giving it any rest. When the wheat crop is hardly gathered he would soon be making the field ready for the next crop and in this hurry all the leftovers from wheat instead of being collected and properly disposed of (as was done earlier now began to be burnt right on the field, thus sending signals of environment pollution in the surrounding areas. And with several fields undergoing such experience the situation soon got alarming leading to several side effects on the rural population and thus posing health problems.

Two major fallouts from such practice which is equally repeated after paddy cultivation when hurriedly paddy straws are burnt to prepare fields for wheat cultivation, are : (a) rise in mosquitoes leading to high incidence of malaria, and (b) rise in respiratory diseases particularly among old people and children. Practically for two months in a year such atmospheric pollution disturbs the rural areas which can be seen at low levels in the shape of smog.

Not only this. High consumption of water for paddy cultivation has led to its reckless withdrawal from underground with the help of tubewells, thus disturbing the water table. As well as several areas with careless use of irrigation facilities have become waterlogged and in this process vast stretches of agricultural land are now lost being permanently submerged under standing water where the drainage cost is stupendous.

The result is that farmers who cultivated these lands recklessly with their latest machinery and used heavy doses of fertilisers and insecticides to maximise their revenue in minimum time without weighing the adverse consequences, are now in a state of shock. Not only this. To finance their grow-rich projects they have borrowed heavily from the state agencies as well as private parties, particularly *Arhtiyas* and now when these loans run into lakhs of rupees they are unable to return them, not even in a position to pay interest charges which in case of private parties are quite high; the latter keep on constantly harassing them with all possible threats.

Little surprise that under such conditions we are told that quite a few farmers have been forced to take the worst step of ending their lives.

This is the most unfortunate and negative fall out from green revolution, particularly the result of quick rise in paddy cultivation where it is estimated that more than 50 per cent of land during summer is under its plough and 70 per cent of rice is disposed of in the national market. Thus, it offers highly alluring alternative crop for income earning to an average farmer and he is thus unlikely to give it up even if alternative and equally viable crop—which appears to be difficult to find despite efforts made by the PAU farm scientists. Thus, this problem of large scale cultivation of paddy which had led to high social fallout in rural areas and disturbed the ecology of this area, when it is estimated that if Punjab continued to follow this pattern of cultivation then during the next few decades much of this area would be turned into permanent wasteland should be tackled with great care through concerted efforts on several fronts to encourage the most feasible and environment friendly land-use. It also calls for wide scale encouraging measures like agro-processing (more value-added to crops), cultivation of vegetables and diversifying into areas like dairy, poultry, horticulture, floriculture and other allied areas.

Most important is that there is need for creating social awareness among the farmers through audio-visual, television and other programmes about the harm that was being done by the reckless withdrawing of underground water which was effecting them and their families as well as neighbours because of their quick rich growing attitude which in fact had backfired and made them loser ultimately. Certainly if these measures are tried there would be a good deal of change in the working pattern of farmers.

8. Green Hazard in Punjab

In the months of October and November one can see clouds of smog hanging low over a vast area of the countryside which spell danger to environment and health particularly that of old people and children.

It was through paddy that Punjab had entered the second phase of green revolution which even surpassed the earlier phase of wheat revolution with faster output and income growth. Indeed the Punjab farmers got so much addicted to this crop that they made big forays into costly new technology so that they were able to reap the maximum benefit. For this, they went in for big loans at high interest rates. So long as the going was comfortable they did not mind heavy payments for these loans.

Infact with growing prosperity they were tempted to raise further loans to celebrate on a lavish scale social ceremonies in the family. New prosperity had encouraged them to lead a life of luxury and extravagance.

Indeed an average farmer in Punjab started comparing himself to his western counterpart. And close to it he was. With new look houses, fitted with the latest gadgets, vehicles for the joy ride of their children, frequent liquor parties and what not.

Lately however this prosperity had begun to delude them for with rising output of paddy they have been finding it difficult to market it. In fact, even the state and central governments, despite commitment, have failed to come to their rescue. While new paddy prices are announced at which the government agencies are supposed to buy but then looking at bulging stocks already lying with them and with hardly any space to accommodate new purchases, they try to find one excuse for the other to keep away from the market.

This has been precisely the situation lately. While farmers converge to different *mandis* with big loads of their crop, they find it extremely difficult to sell. In fact not able to wait indefinitely and their please to the government agencies having completely failed, they are forced to resort to distress sales where prices are more than 30 per cent below the minimum prices announced by the Centre, which of course under the circumstances have no meaning.

Thus farmers are caught in a vicious circle. With big loans yet to be cleared and not even able to pay high interest charges and alternative avenues not available which could fetch them higher income than what they get from paddy, they are forced to raise maximum paddy from their fields.

In fact recently there has been talk that Punjab could even raise two crops of paddy in addition to the usual wheat crop. Thus, it means additional pressure on limited resources as well as on local environment which is otherwise not fit for large-scale paddy cultivation. With limited monsoon this area has to depend on underground water and with maximum land under paddy cultivation one can well imagine how much of underground water has to be drawn to feed the hungry paddy fields.

All this has brought out the problem of fast depletion of underground water resources as well as severe problem of waterlogging rendering a large chunk of agricultural land unfit for cultivation.

In fact this has multiplied the woes of farmers who have lost their land and find themselves helpless in the matter with no alternative avenues to earn income. With big loans awaiting to be cleared and mounting family responsibilities they find the going quite difficult. Little surprise that under these circumstances quite a few farmers have been forced to commit suicide.

Also another major fallout from this excessive cultivation of paddy has been that after the crop is raised farmers are in a hurry to prepare their fields for the winter wheat crop.

In this process they burn their paddy straw and other leftovers right on their fields which result in virtual smog conditions around the villages.

In the months of October and November one can see clouds of smoke hanging low over a vast area of the countryside which spell danger to environment and health particularly of old people and children.

Besides raising a new crop on as yet wet fields leads to multiplication of mosquitoes and consequently a large number of villagers suffer from malaria with one of the highest incidence in the country.

Thus, when inventory is prepared of the cost-benefit of paddy cultivation one would come across a sorry picture and would possibly not favour further rise in its cultivation, rather welcome gradual slow down.

But in the absence of alternative viable crop to replace paddy, farmers would not like to shift.

Even the efforts made by the scientists at the Punjab Agricultural University to encourage alternative environment friendly crops have not been successful because of the uncertain market situation for these crops.

This issue however should be taken use with utmost care and earnestness by farm scientists and other interested agencies so that alternative and more successful solution is found out for curtailing paddy cultivation.

SECTION 4

FOOD STORAGE

9. Rural Godowns : Facility Nearer Home

While rural godowns near home play important role in the storage of foodgrains of small and medium farmers and this save them the hardship of either storing it at home or sell it at unremunerative prices, there has been unfortunately very little attention paid to their construction in rural areas. Now there appears to be positive move to construct them and thus help the harassed farmers in their storage needs. Also there is move to improve technology. One hopes that this programme makes a good progress.

A move is a foot again to revive the system of rural godowns. These had been created with much zeal, particularly in Punjab, during the late 1970s and early 1980s in the wake of the Green Revolution. It was strongly felt that the basic inputs like fertilisers, seeds, and insecticides should be easily available to farmers right at their doorsteps. With this in view it was decided to create a network of rural godowns at the potential centres.

These were developed as focal points to serve the needs of the surrounding 10 to 12 villages. Kind of concrete sheds were created to protect various inputs that could now be easily available as per farmers' needs without difficulty and also at subsidised prices.

The system was encouraged by the state cooperative department that undertook the construction of these godowns with financial assistance from the State and the Centre and also kept them supplied with various inputs.

Failure

Unfortunately, the system was not able to make much headway for certain deficiencies. Foremost, they were created at a time when militancy had started showing its ugly head. The decade saw the peak of militancy, which severely affected the functioning of these godowns. In fact, quite a few of them were even used by militants as hiding places. Besides, not sufficient attention paid to their design, functioning and maintenance. For instance, most of these godowns happened to be too small for any effective service. Also the location was not well thought out.

It also became evident that because of poor management serious pilferage of the stocks in these godowns was a routine. The concept soon lost its shine and the investment made did not yield the desired result.

However, it had helped set a healthy tradition of storage of inputs for farmers so that they did not need to travel great distances. The exercise also provided a lesson for future effective development of such storage places.

It is in this background that an attempt is now being made by NABARD in reviving this system of rural godowns. Funds are now being assured to the prospective parties both in the private sector as well as the state corporations for the improvement of existing godowns as well as construction of new ones as per the experience already gained. Also, to encourage this scheme, subsidy is also being provided to the parties undertaking the job, whether individually or in groups.

Now in view of high pressure on the storage of foodgrains in large godowns, where huge stocks are lost for lack of proper storage, it is expected that the emergence of new rural godowns would help solve the problem.

Apart from providing storage for farmers produce this system would also keep a close watch on the produce.

Effective Design

For promoting effective use, it would be essential to introduce structural changes and the use of superior material in the godowns to make them weather proof, especially during the rainy season. Their management would have to be more alert to discourage pilferage. As economic viability of these godowns depends on their size, it would be essential to go in for the optimum size that has sufficient space for stocking both the produce as well as essential inputs.

We would also have to keep in view the future shape of things when the country goes in for more and more agri-processing activities. It would be useful to involve panchayats in the project. They should also be encouraged to take benefit from NABARD's scheme and construct godowns in their villages which might even gain more prominence than godowns constructed by outside parties. In fact, fear has been expressed that in view of the past not-too-happy experience of rural godowns and the hesitation of the rural population to take to them readily, the new experience might not gain much success and might even prove an exercise in futility.

Thus, it would be essential to ensure the participation of local bodies that would take a long-time interest in the effective functioning of these godowns. A cautious approach would be needed towards so that the project serves the purpose over a long period.

10. State of Foodgrain Storage

Overtime with steady growth of food production there has also occurred enormous demand for capacity for safe storage. Unfortunately this has not been happening. The existing facility is hardly sufficient for the storage of a part of food stocks thus forcing good quantity to be temporarily stored in unsafe and less protected areas thus leading to high wastage and pilferage. It is time that the whole mechanism of storage was reviewed and latest technology introduced which would increase the life of foodgrains.

Already freshly harvested stocks of wheat and converged on the markets and grown into bigger heaps, thanks to the encouraging performance during the *rabi* season. This situation has been repeating over the past 10 years, and is quite unlike the earlier years when there used to be a fairly defined cycle of plenty followed by that of scarcity. If such mood continues, and one hopes so, we would soon need a relook at our entire bufferstock strategy.

Talking of statistics, it is found that at present the FCI godowns numbering around 1,600 in the country have already a stock of around 12.8 million tones of what against the buffer and operational stock norm of 4 million tonnes. Thus, the situation is already grim and would grow grimmer soon with this season's procurement of foodgrain expected to be all-time high.

Though we might feel smug with such a generous situation which would help to tide over even the worst possible food situation in the country and no longer it would be at the mercy of foreign countries which often we had been during the early years of post-Independence period, simultaneously, however, we cannot overlook the heavy cost that has to be incurred both on maintenance as well as management of mind boggling stocks of foodgrain.

In fact, it is found that even after getting a supplementary subsidy of Rs. 944 crore the FCI, the principal stocking agency of foodgrain in the country, is finding the situation still quite grim. And let us not forget the fact that the storage problem is not only of wheat it is equally of rice. It is estimated that when added to the existing stocks of the FCI the fresh stocks of wheat and rice purchased this year, the total would amount to around 42 million tonnes.

One can well imagine the amount of resources needed to manage this job. And yet we would not be able to ensure the safety of stored grain where quite a significant amount is going to be lost through pilferage as well damaged by weather and eaten by pest, thus adding significantly to the country's financial stake.

Under these circumstances there is hardly any justification to go on accumulating these stocks without any planning. The situation has already come to such a pass that it would be advisable to get rid of earlier stocks even if that meant suffering a loss which is surely going to be lower than the additional cost suffered through their further storage.

No surprise under such complex system made worse through announcing high minimum procurement prices mainly to please the farming lobby, the government should be selling wheat at Rs. 900 a quintal, while good quality wheat is available in the open market at Rs. 700 a quintal. What a big difference! which shows that the entire system of creation of bufferstock should have a rational approach.

First, for easing burden on national as well state storage facilities shouldn't we prepare a blueprint for creating alternative storage facilities in the rural area, which being close to farmers would be welcome by them as well reduce pressure on major storage centres located mainly in urban areas.

In fact at one time rural godowns had been encouraged. For instance, in Punjab during the 1970s a large number of rural godowns were built. But these failed to take-off mainly because of poor construction, unplanned location, lack of proper supervision and management.

These godowns could be brought to use again after due changes. New godowns could be designed in such a manner that they win the acceptability of farmers. Further the government should encourage the entry of the private sector into this area by offering suitable sops.

In view of high cost incurred as well as wastage faced, it would be advisable to encourage storage of foodgrain in central and state warehouses only. Here carry over of earlier stocks should be discouraged and got rid of before the fresh stocks start coming. As it has been suggested earlier, even if some loss has to be incurred it would be wise to incur than to face much bigger liability later.

The system of staggering food sales should be adopted to reduce burden on their stocking as well as for realising better prices by the farmers. Currently nearly 90 per cent of foodgrain—equivalent to their total market sales—arrive in the market within a period of two months of harvesting (in the case of wheat April and May and in the case of rice September and October).

Thus, these months turn out to be the busiest periods and

impose the maximum pressure both on the market as well as storage capacity. If we could, with appropriate mechanism, stagger these sales over a longer period it would help farmers to realise better prices and reduce pressure on storage where we are already facing difficult situation.

We should, therefore, develop a functional alternative system which would help both small and medium farmers who are generally forced to bring their produce earlier to the market, to develop their own storage capacity at home as well as have access to larger storage capacity built by each village panchayat as per its needs.

In fact now with the creation ot a network of panchayats in the country it would be advisable to involve them to help farmers in finding more friendly storage facility for their surplus grain as well as such capacity could also be used for storing other products of farmers.

By now it has been sufficiently recognised that in several areas in the country, particularly Punjab and Haryana, agriculture has already reached the saturation limit. We should now concentrate more and more on areas that help farmers to diversify into alternative and more income-yielding activities. This has also been the experience of other advanced countries and they have over the time reduced their manpower engaged in agriculture and put it on more income-yielding avenues as well as this system has helped better allocation of resources and technology in the farm sector itself to raise its productivity.

There is much to be learnt from the experience of these countries to reorganise our agriculture for obtaining higher yields and income as well make better use of the storage capacity already created in the country at a heavy cost.

SECTION 5

FOOD SURPLUS AND DIVERSIFICATION

11. Going Beyond Paddy-Wheat Cycle

The concept of minimum support price should have been discontinued from 1991 as the country is facing the burden of surplus. Support price in agriculture, at least in the case of wheat and paddy, should be discouraged as early as possible. This alone would force farmers to divert their attention to alternative farm activities and move away from the paddy-wheat cycle, which is no longer needed to such an extent.

After the partition, India had lost its food bowl to Pakistan and soon found itself in high deficit necessitating large import of grants from the USA under the PL 480 arrangement. The payment was to be made in rupees thus saving the country from the burden of scarce foreign exchange. With frequent droughts the situation worsened, particularly from mid-1950s to mid-1960s, when large quantity of food had to be imported. This arrangement also helped the USA to dispose of surplus food and it was also able to push into service a large number of its cargo ships to transport food to India. But this arrangement had its adverse impact on our agriculture when Punjab had shown good progress in grain production and faced difficulty in competing with the cheap imported grains. This also acted as a barrier to the growth of our agriculture sector. A way out of this situation was found through adopting Price Support Policy (PSP) of domestic output to make it competitive with imported food and thus had begun the PSP system in the country. The dependence on imported grain was declined after the 1971 Indo-Pakistan war, when USA played a pro-Pakistan role and thus became self-sufficient. This was the major step for boosting farm revolution in Punjab in particular when the 1970s proved to be the best period for farming.

The farm prosperity was at its peak yielding high revenue to farmers who invested a good part in purchasing the latest farm machinery, installation of tubewells and on other similar activities. Further, besides enjoying high prosperity in wheat production, they also entered in a big way in the field of paddy revolution as well.

Much of this revolution was due to continuous high support prices they enjoyed in both the crops which in return helped the empty food bowls of the Centre and state governments. In fact, a large quantity of the FCI godowns were filled with surplus food from Punjab. But such a situation of plenty in Punjab also had its adverse impact. An average Punjabi farmer spent his earnings lavishly, instead of saving for the future. Often he overspent thus running into borrowing from *Arhtiyas* in particular.

His over dependence on paddy cultivation had led to extensive waterlogging and he also faced other calamities. When he could not meet the claims of his creditors and could no longer support his family, he even was driven to commit suicide. His woes have multiplied when lately he has found it difficult to realise good prices for his products, which are not in proportion to the money he has invested on inputs.

Thus having not been taught in farm economics and accountancy he has found himself in adverse situation when neither the government nor *Arhtiyas* are able to compensate him for his bulging deficit, despite the fact that Minimum Support Price (MSP) had been steadily rising even during the period when the market had been invaded with surplus.

With such high accumulated surplus, it is becoming difficult for the government to manage it even through export when cheaper grains are available from other sources. Now in fact with over 60 million tonnes of grain surplus—equivalent to three times the normal surplus needed for the country—we are faced with a gloomy situation when we have to spend nearly Rs. 10,000 crore annually just to care for the stocks, much of which if not cleared in time would become unfit for human consumption.

Under these circumstances, a moot question arises why did we encourage Minimum Support Price (MSP) system beyond the period it was needed? It should have been discontinued at least from 1991 when the country adopted the policy of structural reforms and open markets.

It is also found that the maximum surplus of foodgrains had emerged during this decade when the country was blessed with encouraging monsoon year after year. And interestingly it is during this period again that there had been continuous rise in MSP which in case of paddy works to average Rs. 20. So roughly Rs. 200 was added to each quintal of paddy sold during last fiscal. Thus Imagine what a high burden it has been for the country and also add how much expenditure has been incurred for maintaining large stocks of foodgrains year after year which are now proving to be a burden.

Interestingly, one of the reasons for the Centre sticking to the same price for paddy this year (Rs. 530 per quintal) as of last year has been to discourage farmers from producing more paddy and take to alternative environment friendly and scarce crops like oilseeds, pulses and others where they have announced higher MSP. Rather an unbecoming step particularly at a time when farmers have undergone one of the worst drought situations in recent years and were looking forward to much higher price.

Looking more closely, it was also during this decade that a thoughtless policy of free power and free irrigation which was implemented by the previous Akali-BJP government had stayed in power for its full term. This has been another factor which, besides causing a heavy loss to the state exchequer, also had encouraged farmers to produce the maximum quantity of paddy in particular. It is thus time to have a rational approach to our agriculture. Support price in agriculture—at least in case of wheat and paddy—should be discouraged as early as possible. This alone would force farmers to divert their attention to alternative farm activities and move away from the paddy-wheat cycle which is no longer needed to such an extent. Besides, it would be essential that subsidy provided to present to the units producing fertilisers should be rationalised and gradually done away with.

If need arises, only small and marginal farmers, who have unfortunately failed to benefit from the existing output structure of wheat and paddy, could be supported by other suitable means, but such support should be for limited period. Ultimately, it is the prevalence of market forces that would help the emergence of an appropriate farm scenario. The government should take steps to encourage such a situation.

Also there is urgent need for properly educating farmers both in undertaking more of value adding farm product as well as in making productive use of their saving. The harassment that they had faced recently could have been avoided if they had learnt to control wasteful expenditure and put their earnings in banks, especially during the period when they were enjoying boom situation.

12. Coping with Food Surplus

The bumper harvest of foodgrains in the country can best be utilised through payment of wages in kind mainly to workers employed in rural capital formation activities like construction of roads and digging of irrigation channels. In other words, such gainful employment avenues would open opportunities for those who are currently without regular employment or are earning meagre wages not sufficient to buy grains and other daily needs, and at the same time it would help to develop rural infrastructure in communication, irrigation and other vital areas.

Indian agriculture perhaps never has had such a long spell of favourable weather as it had during the last 10 years without break which has boosted its food situation. Earlier normally 2/3 years of good monsoons would generally end up with drought which necessitated the government to follow a more cautious policy towards storing of grains. Such storage even otherwise was needed to meet the demand from perpetually deficit areas whose demand during lean years would further rise.

It was to safeguard against such uncertain situation that the government had enacted legislation against movement of grains, encouraged their purchase at predetermined prices so that enough stocks were available in central and state godowns. Particularly the FCI was created as principal food storage agency to ensure that sufficient stocks of grains were available at nodal distribution points to tide over any adverse situation, as well as to ensure regular flow of stocks under the public distribution system. Also it was against such background that exports of grains were prohibited.

The situation during the last decade has however been very different with bumper harvest resulting in ever rising pressure on storage where limited capacity made it difficult for storing. Under these conditions it was but natural that a large quantity of grains are stored in the open which has caused considerable damage and rendered a large quantity unfit for human consumption.

This loss runs into several hundred crores of rupees. And the irony is that while this is happening a large number of people are suffering from malnutrition and do not possess enough purchasing capacity to buy grains.

Surely something is wrong with the system and calls for

rethinking to restore balance in stocks of grains up to the safe limit and use the excess available for meeting the consumption need of the people below the poverty line.

And this can be best ensured through payment of wages in kind mainly to workers employed in rural capital formation activities like construction of roads, digging of irrigation channels and undertaking allied activities. In other words, such gainful employment avenues would open opportunities for those who are currently without regular employment or earning meagre wages not sufficient enough to buy grains and other daily needs, and at the same time it would help the rural areas to narrow down gaps in communication, irrigation and other vital areas.

Further to help workers to cash their daily wages into kind, support should be forthcoming from the public distribution system which by now covers practically all rural areas where additional grains as per the requirement over their normal needs could be stored and made available to workers employed on capital formation activities, where they could surrender their coupons against daily wages issued by the authorities and obtain their requirement of grains and other essential items.

In other words, at the end of the day workers would be issued coupons which though would record their daily wages in rupees but these would be encashable at public distribution shops to meet their daily needs, apart from grains a few other essential items would also be available.

Thus, this system would help them to have access not only to grains even other essential items of daily needs the arrangements for these should also be made with these shops. To facilitate smooth functioning of this system more shops would have to be opened as well as manpower needs of existing shops would have to strengthened. This in itself would result in more jobs to be created.

It should not be mandatory that workers collected their requirements every day. They could do so at convenience when their family members could visit these shops during the day time and get the required items after the surrender of coupons.

As the system works and workers' basic needs are adequately met, it could subsequently be converted into part payment in cash and part payment in kind. Thus, in addition to their ration needs workers could also buy other items from the open market against cash received. As well as a system of thrift should be encouraged where a part of cash received could be regularly collected and deposited in the post office account of individual concerned to meet emergent situations.

As by now panchayats have started functioning practically in every village, we should also use this institution to help in the functioning of food security system where each panchayat should be enabled to create its own food storage facility. This would not only help to meet emergent situation, it would also help to cut down heavy cost incurred at present in constructing mega storage facilities as well as on their maintenance and management which currently run into several hundred crores of rupees.

With the functioning of such decentralised system of storage the pressure on central and state godowns would be substantially reduced leading to high saving in cost as well as better distribution of grains. The staff rendered surplus in this way could be easily absorbed in the expanding operation of public distribution system, as outlined earlier.

It is well-known that one of the principal factors obstructing the growth of rural areas is their poor communication network even after 53 years of independence. As massive cost is involved in creating this system, by deploying manpower below the poverty line under the scheme of capital formation outlined above the country would be able to tackle this complex problem to a large extent and thereby reduce the urban-rural gap. This has also been a very major factor in discouraging the globalisation process in reaching down to the rural areas. Fortunately, surplus grains had started emerging right from the time the country entered the globalisation phase which has helped to keep down the cost of living for an average family. If this safety net had not been available one can well imagine its adverse impact on the gains from globalisation. Surely this system of globalisation could be made even more functional and beneficial through opening the frontiers of our rural areas through improving the network of communication system, as explained earlier. The above exercise of course constitutes bare contours—board guidelines—of the programme which needs to be further spelt out in details to make it operational.

Thus, it is the more positive approach to food surpluses which would (a) help their reaching down to the poorest of the poor by putting them in productive jobs of capital formation; (b) raise their earning capacity for providing access to these surplus grains which with enhanced purchasing power they would no longer find it difficult to buy; (c) reduce their malnutritional level and thereby encourage them to lead more healthy and purposeful life; (d) help the rural areas in creating essential capital assets the absence of which is currently responsible for their isolation as well as low farm productivity; and (e) help the nation in cutting down a very large unproductive expenditure incurred at present in maintaining large buffer stocks of grains for which there is not enough space. Thus, the programme of rural capital formation if carefully worked out would yield long-term capital gain to the country and most importantly it would provide very essential capital assets in rural areas the lack of which is currently responsible for their backwardness and poverty, as well as denying them the benefits of globalisation.

13. Diversify Farm Activities

The small and marginal farmers in Punjab are not only living in penury, but are also reducing the area under green cover and forests to unsafe level. One major remedy is to create alternative employment avenues for the family members in activities including mushroom cultivation, floriculture, selected vegetable growing, pisciculture and horticulture.

While population of small and marginal farmers has been bulging, currently estimated over one-third of total population of the country and nearly 50 per cent of the rural population, hardly any tangible and sustainable income-yielding programmes have been planned for this vast section. The result is that majority of them fall below the poverty line and again a substantial number of these fall to the poorest category with income barely sufficient to meet their both ends.

It is heartening to see such a situation in leading agricultural area of the country which has witnessed a lasting thrust of green revolution power. Here obviously the reference is to Punjab which was the first state in the country to usher in a green revolution and thus break the vicious circle of food scarcity and heavy imports and is at the moment responsible for filling of the brim all the godowns of the FCI. But ironically, the number of small and marginal farmers in this state has been fast rising. Of course, it is the result of growing pressure of rural population leading to sub-division of already small holdings which are economically no longer viable. It is estimated that quite a large chunk of area—and just think that already nearly 85 per cent of land in Punjab is under plough, which has reduced area under green cover and forests to an unsafe level, has already been sub-divided into uneconomic holdings which do not yield sufficient income to their owners.

A study done sometime back by Punjab Agriculture University (PAU) researchers had brought out the fact that average holding of a small farmer yielded income which was barely sufficient to be compared with the monthly salary of a newly recruited bottom level functionary in the government department. What a irony it is? Thus small farms are not economically viable and studies made have further confirmed that confronted with such a situation, several of these families have either leased their land to medium/large farmers on mostly long-term contracts accepting small rent in return, or else they have sold their pieces wherever possible and taken to alternative low income-yielding professions, including migration to other areas where conditions have been equally worse.

In a nutshell, neither these small farmers are able to earn sufficient income nor they are able to find worthwhile alternative avenues. Such a situation faced by agriculturally prosperous state of Punjab is an appropriate example to show where we are heading to with rising division of already small piece of land. Either this leads to the emergence of a class of better-off farmers through the backdoor who are able to acquire these lands under the lease system or whenever these are cultivated by farmers themselves they face, almost starvation situation—not able to earn enough to lead a minimum sustainable living. The moot question is what is the way out of this vicious circle? How could further division of small farms be avoided? Or else how these could be made economically viable?

However, one thing is certain that with the existing laws and prevailing customs, land is going to be partitioned further with family partitions. This at the same time cannot go on endlessly. One major remedy to avoid this happening is to create alternative employment avenues for the family members where surplus manpower could be conveniently absorbed and pressure on uneconomic farms would lessen which, in turn, would permit fewer members on land to derive higher income with their efforts.

Even this may not prove sufficient with size of land already existing. Thus, it would call for consolidation of small holdings, say through a system of cooperative farming. But then the experience shows that such farming has not generally proved successful for several reasons. However, the main reason for the failure has been the clash of interest between the parties. Thus, if we could encourage pooling of land and other resources among like-minded people with the same level of income and other interests, this system should work. Of course, still it would need a lot of action, encouragement, help and guidance to the cooperative farmers to make it a real success. Also sufficient care would be needed to avoid clash of family interests which can at any time scuttle the whole programme.

Thus cooperative farming without encouraging results even after consolidating small pieces that could be conveniently brought under mechanised cultivation, harvesting and tubewell irrigation and other facilities, would not work. For its success it has to assure farmers a sufficient and sustainable income.

This would call for a radical change in the existing cropping pattern and substituting it with alternative, more income-yielding ones. As well as the limited current farm cycle confined mainly to wheat-paddy crops—though these have been at the root of green revolution in northern India—has proved quite harmful to the ecology of this area and has brought several adverse consequences including high water-logging.

Certainly this system has to be discontinued and replaced by alternative crops and activities which are more environment-friendly and at the same time yield sufficient income.

This is where our farm scientists and departments of agriculture should put their attention. Here we would have to encourage a basket of high income-yielding activities including areas like mushroom cultivation, floriculture, selected vegetable growing, pisciculture, horticulture and the like. But while encouraging these areas, we must be prepared for scientific storage, distribution and marketing. While strategic changes are needed in the existing basket of production in the interest of ecology as well as yielding higher income to farmers, this would only be possible if we have a good package of interrelated services to boost the morale of farmers.

Thus, a lot of home work would be required before we empower small farmers. It should be remembered that future lies more and more in agro-processing activities which help both better preservation of farm and related products for a long time and also would bring forth large employment avenues to the farm population where it is the youngsters who would be able to branch out into newly emerging agro-processing activities.

One of the major reasons for the slow growth of these agro-industries in the country has been the lacklustre approach to these industries adopted by the government as well as the private sector and also due to limited market. That shows we have failed to tap otherwise promising market through regular programmes on the media, demonstrations and sales promotion programmes both in the urban and rural areas, making people aware of the benefits derived from such products which saves the country several hundred crores of rupees lost at present due to high wastage of fruits, vegetables and other farm products when they fall to be scientifically preserved and more so under harsh conditions of our warm climate.

If cost-benefit study were made of such wastage and gain had even through partial preservation we would find that gains overstep loses incurred in such investment. Thus, a package programme of agro-industries should be encouraged where small farmers should be made an integral part of this system.

14. Need to Tap Citrus Fruit Potential

Citrus fruits hold out a high potential in the growth of horticulture industry. While India happens to be world's one of the major producers of several citrus fruits, it has however a very small share in the world fruit trade. Experts should seriously think of measures that were needed to raise the growth of quality citrus and other fruits which competed well in the world market. Also scientific development of our horticulture potential would help diversify farm activity, particularly when we are anxiously looking forward to measures needed to reduce production of crops which have not only reached saturation limit but also are causing environment problem (like rice cultivation).

While India has hitherto by and large concentrated on agriculture and that too mainly on wheat and paddy, it has yet to tap the high growth and value addicting horticulture products where it has considerable advantage in citrus fruits. The main citrus fruits are oranges (both sweet and mandarin varieties), lemons/lime and grape fruits. It is interesting that at one time India was the nursery of citrus fruits grown from time immemorial in Indo-China and sub-Himalayan region of Asia. Now of course they are grown almost everywhere, though there are specific countries which have a larger share, but unfortunately India hardly figures among the big producers which shows the utter neglect on the part of this country to tap the fast growing world market for citrus fruits, especially in developed countries where they commonly figure in their daily consumption.

Interestingly while India is the sixth largest producer of citrus fruits accounting for 5 per cent of global production it has no place in world citrus trade which is due to its sticking to its old varieties with little introduction of new varieties where, for instance, mandarins are now seedless while India yet continues to stick to mandarins which have hardly any market with global consumers. This is due to lack of quality control which plays an important role in exports, little encouragement of international standards and poor marketing practices. Thus, unless these handicaps are removed there is little chance for increasing the share in world demand.

We notice that the highest expansion of improved citrus fruits is taking place in China and Brazil. Thus, it is our neighbour China, like in so many other areas, that has taken the lead to improve its citrus industry which fetches it a very rich dividend.

In the current 94 million tonnes of export of citrus fruits it is the sweet orange that occupies 71 per cent share, followed by the tangerine variety (13 per cent), lime and lemon (10 per cent) and grape (6 per cent). Brazil is the world's largest producer of citrus frozen orange juice, while Spain is the largest exporter of fresh citrus fruits. Japan, though the largest producer of the mandarin variety, hardly exports. Thus, almost all of it is consumed in the domestic market.

In India, the production of citrus fruits is around 3.8 million tonnes. It is the mandarin variety which has the largest share, followed by sweet orange and acid lime—their share is 41, 23, 23 per cent, respectively. In terms of area under citrus fruits it is Maharashtra that tops (over 73,000 hectares), Andhra Pradesh (56,200 hectares), Punjab (37,500 hectares), Karnataka (34,400 hectares), UP and Bihar (22,500 and 17,300 hectares, respectively. However, in terms of production we meet a different picture. It is the highest in Tamil Nadu, followed by Madhya Pradesh, Gujarat, Andhra Pradesh and Bihar, respectively.

It shows that area under cultivation does not bear any relationship to productivity where there is a considerable scope to raise it. And, of course, compared to global picture, productivity of citrus fruits in India is very low. Thus, both quality as well as productivity need to be carefully upgraded through rigorous R & D programme.

Another area where we have to devote our attention is to cut down heavy losses suffered annually due to lack of cold storage and modern processing facilities. Besides improving quality and productivity, it would be also essential to improve storage and processing facilities for citrus fruits. In a country like Brazil it is sweet orange processed industry which enjoys global shine. For instance, it is estimated that this industry is responsible for earning over $ 1 billion revenue annually and generate nearly half-a-million job opportunities.

Our technologists would have to learn a lot from this Latin American country. The government should also invite experts from this and other fast growing countries to improve our current low status in the citrus fruit industry.

15. Exploit the Potential of Mushrooms

Besides alternative crops, which are good income yielders and more acceptable by farmers, we need to tap other areas of the economy such as mushroom cultivation, which are found favourable particularly with small farmers and landless labourers. While India has been traditionally a major mushroom growth country, we have not tried to exploit its potential in the global market.

India has by now, thanks to successful functioning of green revolution for the past more than three decades, reached the advance stage of food production where it is able to generate surplus so much so that it doesn't have sufficient space for its storage resulting large stocks running into several lakh tonnes exposed to high damage. Thus, the green revolution has also resulted in rather adverse consequence of such unplanned growth where we do not have sufficient plans either to dispose of such stock in the international market or have plans of processing which could convert surplus into high value products.

Also we must admit the harmful consequence being faced through growth of certain crops against the natural capacity of the soil. This had obvious reference to a crop like paddy which has occupied extraordinary attention in the north-western states of Punjab and Haryana which are otherwise not suited for such activity. But its high commercial gains make the farmers to grow it in a large quantity. The result has been high damage to ecology with underground water table receding sharply in several areas.

While the government is aware of the situation, it has been quite slow in tackling it. The often talked of remedy to tackle this situation has been diversification of the farm economy replacing much of paddy land by alternative crops which are more environment friendly. But here the problems faced are : (a) slow emergence of alternative environment, friendly crops where the research already undertaken in the farm universities has not resulted in viable solutions, and (b) the alternative crops that have been encouraged are not economically viable (where both productivity as well as marketing pose big problems). Thus, the farmers are slow to adapt alternative crops and continue to stick to paddy.

The situation calls for more aggressive and planned strategy on the part of the government. Besides alternative crops, which are good income yielders and more acceptable by farmers, we also need to tap other areas of the economy which are found favourable particularly with small farmers and landless labourers whose number has been steadily rising and whose income is declining. These one-third of the country's population need to be brought in a circle of productive activity where they can look to sustained, viable and growing income. Simultaneously, we must also look into the problems of large players, as it is the combined effort of both large and small producers would bring long-term prosperity to the country. Apart from all other crops, mushroom cultivation promises high return. While India has been traditionally major mushroom growing country in the world, we have so far paid only lip service to tame it for earning income in the global market. We still continue to hold a very small share in the world market, where mushroom is estimated to be growing at the annual rate of 25 per cent. Its demand is high in the western countries who are drawn to its high nutritional contents.

As far as return obtained from per unit land of mushroom cultivation, it is estimated that one could have a return of Rs. 6.2 lakh within five months on a small plot of 1000 sq. yards by investing Rs. four lakh. This just gives an idea of high income that can be earned through systematic cultivation of mushrooms. Further it doesn't require any arable land for cultivation as it can be grown inside room on various farm wastes, dry leaves, etc. Also the produce of mushrooms has a good market and unlike floriculture it is a low volume high value product and doesn't require fresh marketing. Thus, if we can create appropriate environment for the growth of quality mushrooms through proper awareness, inputs and training of our people who are also offered suitable credit and marketing facilities, we should be able to create good income for them.

Interestingly it is China, our neighbour, which has been shrewd enough to take advantage of the situation and encouraged cultivation and marketing of mushrooms on an extended scale. Currently it occupies almost one-third share of global market which is indeed remarkable. As fresh mushroom have a very short shelf life, a very large international trade is in processed form. This is all the more so in case of India where its domestic market for fresh mushrooms is very small. Thus, we have to by and large which needs to be tapped by the government through systematic effort.

Thus, here we have a golden opportunity to exploit the fast growing international market for the processed mushrooms. Why should India not be able to do so? provided we take positive steps both for scientific cultivation and processing of our mushrooms. This should also provide the best opportunity to the state beleaguered with excess stocks of foodgrains and frantically looking for alternative activities.

Besides, we should also encourage the consumption of fresh mushrooms in the local market which has a high nutritional contents.

SECTION 6

RURAL DEVELOPMENT AND PANCHAYATS

16. Focus on Rural Development

The development of basic rural facilities would itself have created a large number of labour-intensive jobs for the rural population and so it would have been the case in several other areas. The only remedy for this situation is to give a high priority to rural development programmes like Gram Sadak Yojana.

Sometime back, the former Prime Minister Atal Behari Vajpayee had expressed his great concern for the neglect of labour-intensive technology under the race for globalisation and structural reforms. In fact, our structuralists have been quick in adding that if India was to compete effectively in the world market it must manufacture the latest products which embody the latest (highly capital-intensive) technology, which has hardly any place for labour-intensive technology, notwithstanding the fact that the labour situation in this country is yet by and large quite different from the advanced economies. Most of our labour force, despite emergence of technical training institutes, is still unskilled and does not possess even elementary knowledge of modern technology. Little surprise therefore that several of them have failed to find employment in the new plants.

While some part of capital-intensive technology was performed by our unskilled and semi-skilled workers, now with the emergence of modern technology there is no longer any such scope with the result that several workers are finding it hard to adjust to the new industrial environment.

It is also observed that even in the current approach to agriculture, small farmers are being driven away with the emergence of land-use for more productive and high income-yielding crops needing scientific cultivation and management of farms of viable sizes where small farmers are absolutely unequal to the job. Thus, with little compensation offered these poor farmers are forced to seek alternative avenues of employment.

Consequently several of them have been driven to crowd the urban population which is quite evident from the fast rising urbanisation where it has been estimated that by 2050 it would rise to 50 per cent. In other words, half of the country's population would have embraced urbanisation.

Imagine the situation that this country would be facing then with poor scenario of basic facilities quite evident from the current plight of several urban areas which have almost turned into big slums, lacking even elementary facilities, face severe shortage of shelter, water and sanitation facilities. And the worst situation is of pollution.

Thus, the current mode of production is not what our earlier leaders looked to find after Independence. Their dreams were quite different—a balanced development of country's resources, keeping balance between rural and urban development, balance between labour-intensive and capital-intensive technology so that the country enjoyed the quality of life that made its population live happily and contented.

Nothing of this sort has unfortunately happened. In fact, soon after Independence—and more so after the assassination of Mahatma Gandhi in January 1948, the leaders had practically forgotten such type of balanced development and instead adopted a strategy that had gradually turned into more capital-intensive. That is also quite apparent from our industrial policy statements where it was the capital-intensive mode of production that was given the pride of place.

Look at how this country chose the path of public sector where much of our previous resources began to be the quickly invested like in basic and heavy industries, notwithstanding the fact that we lacked miserably in basic infrastructure facilities and technically trained manpower as well as possessed very limited resources.

Unfortunately these areas were badly neglected and instead we adopted a strategy that created a severe imbalance in our growth.

Also long-term emphasis on heavy industry was uncalled for when India possessed reasonably efficient private sector in quite a few areas who if properly encouraged could have done the job far better and saved the country of such wasteful expenditure.

We had adopted a socialistic pattern of development where we wanted key industries like steel, mining, heavy electrical and other key industries exclusively in the public sector which we thought was the right course of development in our country, though ultimately as it is well-known we failed miserably and ran into losses and failures.

Had this country's scarce resources been utilised in alternative and more productive areas like creation of basic facilities, encouragement of agriculture on a sound footing with the presence of dependable irrigation, modern inputs and other allied facilities we would have not only made this country self-sufficient, we would have also become an important source of export earning.

Instead we had turned into major importer of food for a number of years. Imagine the food situation in the late 1950s and 1960s and even for quite a few years later when we faced severe shortage of food which had led to high suffering for the local population and we had to send several SOS message to food surplus countries for help.

All this could have been avoided if we had followed a sound agriculture policy in time, given pride of the place to irrigation, created rural roads, scientific system of cultivation, inputs and marketing. We failed to develop these facilities for a number of years and even today a good part of the country lacks dependable irrigation, transport and marketing facilities.

Even now the starvation deaths do occur especially in the tribal areas and the country continues to be loaded with a sizeable tribal population who become the first victims whenever there is a drought in the country.

We had been committed to the development of urban areas and neglected the rural areas notwithstanding the fact that our major population still lives in villages.

Even today the rural areas lack in basic facilities, elementary roads, health care or jobs. Little surprise that a major part of our youth had to seek asylum in urban areas. That is how urban pressure had started building up fast.

Had we planned the country's development well we would have created sufficient opportunities for the rural population, particularly in labour-intensive areas. The development of basic rural facilities would have itself created a large number of labour-intensive jobs for the rural population and so it would have been the case in several other areas.

Unfortunately we failed to do so and we should now be prepared to face the exodus of rural population to urban areas in days to come.

The only remedy for this situation is to give a high priority to rural development programmes where the Prime Minister's much publicised programme of Gram Sadak Yojana should itself get a high priority and completed within the minimum possible time and in itself is the source of creating several lakhs of employment avenues for the rural population.

17. Strengthen Panchayat Raj System

The government of India, instead of expanding ministries, should think of more productive alternative channels for proper utilisation of the funds released for rural development. There is a need to strengthen the functioning of panchayats and also Panchayat Raj System.

While every political party tries to stands by its commitment to rural development, even bows several times before the rural folks promising to provide them with ideal governance, but soon voted to power these commitments vanish into thin air. This has been the sad experience of every government since independence. None has been able to stand by their commitments. May be it is the comfort of living in sprawling bungalows as well as posh office from where they govern, make them forget the plight of poor farmers labouring under most difficult conditions in their fields. Hardly any state or Central minister visit the rural areas of their constituencies, thus conveniently forget promises they have made to these people which remain unfulfilled and they continue to be deprived of basic facilities.

Rural people had hoped that these promises would be redeemed under the Panchayat Raj, which was proclaimed to bring the true democratic rule when their destinies would be shaped with liberal help from the Centre and other agencies. But soon they realised it was all farce, and they have remained where they were.

In fact, several panchayats have yet in take-off in the proper sense. While those functioning face high resource crunch and even whatever little amount reaches them is virtually siphoned away by members who wield high influence in the rural power structure, when it is the poor, marginalised and illiterate members who are completely sidelined and practically have no say in the functioning of these bodies.

Nothing has improved even after creation of the democratic local bodies. No leader ever bothers to visit these panchayats much less take interest in their functioning.

It is only a few prominent panchayats that draw their attention and that too for their personal interests. Surely with such lacklustre functioning of panchayats, one can hardly expect the larger interest of the poor farmers even to be cared. Neither a minister meets farmers nor he allows them into his office whenever they approach him.

On the other side, in one place of ministry of agriculture at the Centre there have emerged number of ministries right under it, where of course there is a lot of overlapping. Further one wonders with the emergence of new ministries there has been any effective gain to the rural areas.

In fact, an ordinary villager is completely confused which ministry he has to approach in case of need? Therefore, it is questionable for whose benefit these several ministries have been created by branching out the ministry of agriculture where the exchequer has been hard pressed for releasing a lion's share of government funds.

While several schemes of rural development have been put into operation after such haphazard expansion of ministry of agriculture, the reality is that hardly a small percentage of these reaches the target groups.

The moot question is why this system cannot be improved? Why we cannot think of better alternative to reach the targeted groups and close the doors for all middlemen? of one applies for funds, only 50 per cent of the released amount reaches the organisation.

When this is the state of affairs with educated people, what would be the plight of illiterates. Rajiv Gandhi was quite justified in his remarks for when NGOs were left with 50 per cent of the grant it could not be more than 10 per cent in case of illiterates.

Thus, government of India, instead of expanding ministries, should think of more productive alternative channels for proper utilisation of the released funds. A close watch should be kept on those officers who indulge in corruption. Unfortunately many NGO bodies fail to report against the corrupt officers.

It should also be advisable to strengthen the Panchayat Raj system which should be made solely responsible for types of programmes of rural development and for which they should be provided with sufficient funds.

All panchayats should have experienced employees to maintain accounts and other records in systematic way and also its members should be trained efficiently. Thus, there is need to strengthen the functioning of panchayats than spending funds on the expansion of the ministry.

Section 7

KHADI

18. Khadi Carries World Class Potential

Indian government, in the post-independence era, made sincere efforts to revive the rural industries and in particular Khadi, which employed the maximum number of people. Unfortunately the enthusiasm that was displayed in the early period was largely missing in the subsequent period. Despite the country having a powerful Khadi Commission, it has failed to take care of vital factors and thus we have landed the once reasonably prosperous sector into an era of gradual decline.

After independence India was strictly committed to rural development and especially rural industries, where khadi and allied industries occupied a prime place providing employment to a vast section of rural population. This thinking was also in line with Gandhiji's concern for rural development where he had devoted maximum attention for the growth of rural industries through various means. In fact, in his concept of Purna Swaraj (complete freedom) it were the small scale industries and overall rural development which occupied high priority and on rural development in post-independence era.

True to his wishes the Indian government, in the post-independence era, made sincere efforts to revive the rural industries and in particular Khadi, which employed the maximum number of people. It had started with the introduction of new technology used for Khadi spinning where Ambar Charkha was introduced in place of traditional charkha, which ensured much better and faster spinning of yarn. The rural artisans were encouraged to go in for these charkhas at highly subsidised prices. In fact, liberal loans were provided to enable them to shift to new charkhas. A few other changes were also introduced which vastly improved Khadi production.

For quicker development, Khadi and Village Industries Commission was set-up with its headquarters in Mumbai. A liberal budget was also provided for its functioning and its was duly entrusted with the task of overall development of country's rural industries in a planned and well coordinated manner. The government even provided liberal resources in the central plan for rural industries, in general and Khadi, in particular. It also laid down some restrictions on the growth of mill sector which was the major competitor for Khadi industries to ensure that interests of these Khadi industries were duly protected and much of the additional production that was needed in view of growth, in demand for textiles was duly met through Khadi industries. Even some cess was levied in the mill sector to provide subsidy to the handloom sector so that it could compete effectively with the mill sector.

It was later realised that these steps for the protection of Khadi industries at the cost of more efficient mill sector were damaging the growth of modern industries and thus it was found advisable not to press these steps any further.

Even then the government did its level best for the growth of Khadi and Village Industries. The market problem that artisans were facing to a large extent also was solved through encouragement of sales cooperatives and through starting a chain of Khadi emporiums in urban areas.

Unfortunately the enthusiasm that was displayed in the early period was largely missing in the subsequent period when the government was far more involved in large industries (including basic and heavy industries mostly through public sector programmes) and less attention was devoted to the rural industries. Therein Khadi production suffered a lot. There was hardly any structural change in its mode of production. In fact, after Ambar Charkha, we hardly find any other technology that made its dent in the Khadi sector. In the absence of strong roots and financial support several artisans found it difficult to survive, particularly in the face of well-organised mill and powerloom sectors which had made tremendous advances and with vast advertising machinery and cheaper prices had captured a large segment of the rural market.

Despite the country having a powerful Khadi Commission, it unfortunately has failed to take care of vital factors and thus we have landed once reasonably prosperous sector into an era of gradual decline. Most of the artisans are finding it difficult to survive notwithstanding their special skills and craftsmanship. The younger generation have shifted to alternative areas. There is urgent need for coordinated action to put Khadi back on the Indian map and make it number one industry in the rural areas, where unfortunately alternative job opportunities are fast shrinking; even agriculture, with fast growing rural population, is becoming unremunerative and people are earnestly looking forward to alternative avenues. But lack of alternative non-farm development and poor infrastructure is obstructing the growth of any meaningful industry in these areas. The situation is worse in backward states like Bihar, Orissa, eastern UP, much of MP and Rajasthan.

Here Khadi and other traditional industries still hold much promise. There has to be a facelift and introduction of new technology. New inputs which appeal to customer taste, new designs, appropriate advertisement, concentrated efforts to capture foreign markets where there exists considerable scope, provided it is successfully tapped.

A lot of homework has therefore to be done before we can capture both national and global markets. Here we are fortunate to have Vasundhara Raje as minister of state for small industries who is quite seized of the problem and is keen to put Khadi and other village industries on a level footing with other industries with complete overhauling of their designs, material used, texture and appeal they hold to global customers.

With Centre's liberal funds for rural development there is no shortage of funds. Rather the fear is about the effective utilisation of these funds. Also we do not have experience of disbursement of rural funds when most of these fail to reach the target. We have to develop alternative strategy to reach the target.

The role of Khadi Commission, which still continues to be the main body in development of Khadi and allied areas, should also be closely evaluated and lapses found, need to be properly plugged to make the Commission serve its role more effectively.

Thus, with a new look at the Khadi and other village industries we could certainly turn these into dynamic areas ready to cater to the need of global markets, which hold much promise as people are keen to switch over to alternative, more attractive and comfortable cotton wears.

When initially Japanese entrepreneurs were to introduce their new products and make them popular among people to overseas markets, it was their embassies which played an important role. These also helped in market research to know more scientifically the tastes of foreign buyers. Thus our embassies too, the world over, could play an equally important role in this respect.

There has also to be considerable fecelift in the chain of Khadi and village industries emporiums on which the nation is spending huge amount on their rental and establishment. At present, these hardly serve much purpose. In fact, for most of the time, the salesmen in these emporiums are virtually on holiday with few customers walking into these stores.

Further we have these stores in prime areas where brisk business is done by the private sector. We must change our attitude towards these Khadi centres. Staff them with right type of people who should be smart; active and committed people. Pay them well.

It will pay us in the long-run. Let them also make suggestions in the improvement of these areas and in fact encourage them to become an active partners in their functioning. Reward the energetic and pushing sales people who show good results.

19. New Role Mooted for Khadi Commission

Khadi was considered to have enormous employment potential and practically the only source of alternative employment to the crowded farm sector, in post-independence era. But due to the stress on heavy industry programme in the public sector, it was realised that this programme would take a long time to generate sufficient employment. Hence, the main issue is the need for creating sufficient alternative employment avenues for the rural population and wean them away from the no longer sustainable khadi sector as well as other traditional village industries.

Khadi had a chequered history during more than half a century period of post-independence. Considering its employment potential and practically the only source of alternative employment to the crowded farm sector, it was considered as a new *avatar*, in the changing horizon of India's industrial scenario. Under large basic and heavy industry programme in the public sector, it was realised that this programme would take a long time to generate sufficient employment avenues and even then might not be on a scale to beat India's bulging population.

In fifties and sixties khadi was accorded with special treatment even at the cost of growth of modern textile industry where it was found necessary to peg output to a specific limit under the plan, so that sufficient market was available for the khadi and allied industries.

It was also at the same time realised that Khadi, of traditional variety, would no longer attract the consumer's taste and the prevailing technology would not be able to cope up with new demand where both productivity and improved quality are much needed. Thus new technology resulted in,

Ambar Charkha, which was a vast improvement over the traditional Charkha and other areas of khadi continued to be improved further with changing mood of the market. It helped greatly the earning capacity of a weaver thus bringing him more income.

Along with it, changes occurred in the weaving segment and khadi was more attractive with new designs and other innovations. There was also blending of khadi with modern synthetic fibre thus reducing its maintenance and wear and tear aspects.

And several other changes too occurred; thus encouraging more scientific and modern look to this sector. The areas of management and marketing witnessed considerable change. Thus, khadi was no longer confined to the periphery of rural areas and soon made a big dent in urban areas and even in foreign markets.

Even then, unfortunately, its development could not make a substantial jump and in fact in urban areas it remained confined to basically elite section where demand was very limited and here again had not been for the highly subsidised khadi showrooms set-up in posh localities, it would have been very difficult to capture even this limited demand.

On the other hand, khadi which was basically developed keeping in view of a common man's market, unfortunately did not find favour with him. The end result was that all efforts made to popularise khadi did not find sufficient national market both in rural and urban areas. Thus it faced a paradoxical situation. The government ultimately yielded to the pressure from the mill sector where already artificial support to the khadi sector at the cost of mill sector had done considerable damage to the growth of the latter. After the mill sector was freed from these artificial curbs there was a quick growth in this sector and vast qualitative improvement in its products.

That shows that given the free market situation people would prefer mill products to khadi and other village industries products. Naturally in competitive terms mill products turn out to be both cheaper as well as more attractive and easy to wash and wear. And that suits a common man who thus patronises such goods in preference to khadi.

Thus, evaluation in terms of comparative cost the situation has gone in favour of modern mill sector and left the khadi sector and allied areas far behind. In fact even during the early sixties our Nobel Laureate Amartya Sen's whole research work was based on economics of alternative choice of techniques where he worked out on heavy losses suffered through artificial support of Ambar Charkha and allied activities.

But then, as said above, it was not so much of the economic cost but social cost that was important in case of this country, burdened with large illiterate and unskilled manpower who hardly had any other source of income. Thus even if the nation had to incur social cost in the shape of subsidy to the khadi sector it was worth incurring to keep the wolf of hunger away from the doors of these people.

But then the question arises, how long this subsidy system could be sustained? Particularly so now when the country has, from the last decade, opened its markets to global economy. It has now turned out to be highly competitive where survival is only possible by keeping in touch with the latest technology and knowledge.

Thus the big question that face us now in the khadi sector and other rural industries is how to cope with the new situation, particularly when these industries still continue to provide major support to rural population?

The past decade's experience has been grim in so far as khadi and village industries is concerned. We have not been able to provide worthwhile support to a large number of people affected by the new economy.

We certainly can not remain sitting on the fence and have to make a positive move which is on consonance with changed times.

The main issue is the need for creating sufficient alternative employment avenues for the rural population and wean them away from the no longer sustainable khadi sector as well as other traditional village industries which have witnessed considerable erosion overtime and can no longer be artificially supported when they have failed to stand on their own during the last 50 years.

It is time for serious thinking and working out new framework of rural development without much disturbing the existing handicaps of illiteracy and lack of skill among average rural manpower.

While we have Gram Panchayats active in practically every village—and this has been a big achievement during the past decade,—we have hitherto not used this dynamic institution for changing the economic profile of rural areas. It is well-known that there is a heavy backlog in rural development programme which in fact constitutes the backbone of national development itself.

The reference is obviously to the serious dearth even of elementary infrastructure without which rural-urban duo cannot move in unison. Little surprise most of development hitherto and more so under recent globalisation has remained confined mainly to urban areas.

How can you expect new economy to make deep impact when two-thirds of population is out of its orbit? Sooner the rural areas are made integral part of urban economy better it would be for the whole nation.

And this can only be done through a network of basic infrastructural facilities—rural roads, irrigation channels, drinking water facilities, dispensaries, schools—in fact there is a vast agenda of rural infrastructure to be completed before the nation can make sustainable progress and provide gainful employment to its people.

Here panchayats should be brought to the fore to execute these programmes with both technical and financial assistance which would yield long-term gains. The modalities of this programme should be worked with care and this programme should be carried out under the leadership of panchayats.

Thus, it is no longer khadi industries that should occupy prominent role in rural areas—in fact we should have moved away from them much earlier and in its place encouraged programme as outlined above. It has vast growth potential and generates employment particularly for those who are unskilled and illiterate.

It is therefore time that Khadi and Village Industries Commission Changes to Rural Infrastructure and Technology Commission and thus plays a significant role in these areas which are in consonance with the current policy of globalisation. Its fast penetration into the rural areas should be effectively accomplished by the new role of Khadi and Village Industries Commission.

SECTION 8

CORRUPTION

20. Decline of Indian Polity

Indian democracy is no longer a means to achieve the goal of welfare and progress. It has turned into a discredited institution. The basic cause of occurrence of this sad situation appears to be a gradual decline in the quality of leadership and the corruption.

One of the undesirable fallouts of the Indian brand of democracy has been that the system itself has by and large been used for undemocratic ends. This could surely not have been the purpose behind such democracy. But unfortunately this is what the experience has shown.

Look how sloth in our democracy has set in over time. In the early independence days our leaders had been honest and even though in-experienced in the art of democratic governance, did their best to apply democratic norms in running the administration smoothly which would benefit particularly the masses. Both top leaders and elected representatives and others joined hands to promote clean governance. The people, especially illiterates, had full faith in them and were usually satisfied with the response they got.

Both political leaders as well as bureaucrats were easily accessible to people of all classes. Leaders were honest and committed and in fact the erring officers were soon pulled up.

Surely under such transparent governance there could be a few chances of corruption or the opposition members raising fingers about the honesty and integrity of the members ruling the government. Democracy thus worked in its true sense. But at the same time, it is not true that things did not go wrong in those days. They did and which was natural especially when administration was moving from colonial to democratic era where new norms had to be established.

But then because of honesty of leaders and their genuine concern for the people and commitment to usher in a new regime of transformation of backward economy to a modern one, where a lot of hiatus had to be covered in areas of infrastructure, industrialisation, education and training of young people for taking up new responsibilities that the country's development itself demanded, it was remarkable that we used our democratic system to achieve these goals.

But what went wrong subsequently. The democratic values, its achievements had soon started moving on a downward trend. Its functioning began to wrap more and more in corruption.

Now Indian democracy is no longer a means to achieve the goal of welfare and progress. It had turned into a discredited, institution. We used democratic right of voting merely to select another no less corrupt government. Unfortunately, we hardly had any alternative though we hopefully thought that the next government may prove less corrupt. But in vain.

Why there have been reverses in our earlier values in democratic administration?

The basic cause of occurrence of this sad situation appears to be a gradual decline in the quality of leadership which instead of improving with time has sadly tended to worsen. The upright, sincere and fired with zeal and commitment type of leadership, which we were fortunate to be blessed with earlier, is gradually disappearing.

It appears that the new generation, was not well equipped with values that their predecessors had cultivated. The posterity was not prepared to follow in their footsteps and instead preferred a path of complacency, easy going and self-perpetuation by all possible means thus putting self far more supreme than the country. This negative attitude of not looking beyond self, which was very much shunned by the earlier era leaders when they put the country far more supreme than self has been, I feel, singularly a supreme cause behind steady decline of our leadership.

The emergence of this negative quality has its own background. This has emerged and got strengthened when a class of highly literate people hailing from families who had no axe to grind, began to be replaced by persons lacking such background.

Gradually with the demise of these people there has occurred a big void and soon the national vote bank which instead began to be surged with by a class of people who lacked these qualities. There was little chance of more enlightened people becoming political leaders. And thus those who dominate the government now mostly lack that training, background, education, experience their predecessors possessed. Hence with gradual shift in the vote bank composition there has occurred a leadership imbalance. It has been the emergence of such class dichotomy and with such suddenness that has gradually brought debasement in the value system of democracy.

Look at the political system these days—the composition of MLAs, MPs, ministers both at the Centre as well as states. They are mostly persons who lack sterling qualities that were possessed by their predecessors and unfortunately this system has been declining as more and more 'netas' (leaders) of doubtful integrity and largely self-seekers are taking up the reins of administration, thanks to the magic of number that guides the democratic system.

And in this pure number game the quality of administration has also suffered a serious setback. Compare the present time administration with earlier one. Earlier officers were allowed free hand in administration. There was little interference in the functioning of the top brass unless something went wrong. Infact when there was lack in expected performance the bureaucrat was taken to task and even disciplinary action was taken against him.

Now things have become different. Surely the present type of functioning of the political system where members are largely concerned with their family welfare and are anxious to accumulate wealth by whatever means one cannot expect administration to remain unaffected. In fact often it is noticed that promotions and placements of bureaucrats are very much linked with the equation they enjoy with the political bosses. That shows what quality of administrators are themselves turning out to be.

Whenever there is a change in any state government, the first task that the new chief minister performs is to completely overhaul the top slots in the government. Those bureaucrats who have been closely linked with the earlier governments are shifted to less important slots and those bureaucrats who have been favourably inclined to the new administration or so it appears through their lobbying with the new government or were made victims by the earlier governments, are adjusted into the vacated slots.

Surely under such type of bureaucracy one is made to mend fence with the political bosses in case they want to move to a key position or recommended for a transfer to the Centre. Sadly while it is the taxpayer's money that is spend in paying fat salaries and perks to the bureaucrats, under the political system unfortunately the benefit of their services are generally related to the services they can render to the political bosses. And it is this linkage that has also been a principal factor for corruption.

Various state corporations that are attached to state departments are in fact den of corruption. They are used as convenient sources of garnering funds by those in power. And it is well known that their management is handed over to favourite bureaucrats. The big losses incurred are directly proportional to their mismanagement when large funds disappear into undesirable channels and ultimately they are made to bleed heavily at the cost of exchequer.

Several other schemes run by the Centre and State Governments for the much claimed benefit for the rural people in particular and for which hundreds of crores of rupees are released regularly, are also a rich source of corruption where it is openly admitted that barely 10 to 15 per cent of money actually reach the beneficiaries while the rest of it is siphoned off into the pockets of those who run these schemes.

It is also well-known how the appointment bodies themselves have become a major source of corruption.

The jobs advertised by these bodies are actually sold to the highest bidders and the booty is shared by those who are to make clean selection based on merit! There are several other channels that have been opened to derive the maximum mileage out of the public funds which help the government functionaries right from bottom to top. Almost each politician and bureaucrat is keen to derive the maximum share out of these public resources during their tenure.

To a large extent the blame for encouraging such debasement in values has into small measure also due to elder statesmen failing to take adequate steps for changing the status of the country's teeming millions residing in the rural areas through education, health facilities, training programmes, improvement in the communication network and the like which would have ultimately moulded these people for playing a more positive role in the governance of the country.

It was rather unfortunate that while the country was taking its shape most of its resources were spent only for the development of urban middle classes who got the lion share of aggregate investment in both social and economic overheads.

See the investment made in urban facilities and industrialisation programmes. One and all these programmes were mostly middle class-oriented. This strategy had in due course led to a vast hiatus between the middle class population and the rural poor whose number increased and it is higher than the middle class population.

Thus at a time when we had started with earnestness the programmes of rural development, it was quite late for bridging the harm done already in disturbing the balance between the two segments of population haves and have nots. And for this we are now paying a heavy price in the form of corruption.

21. Official-Politician Nexus

The system of corruption flourishes because of close nexus between officials and politicians. It was quite evident from the recent case of chairman of Punjab Public Service Commission who made crores of rupees by selling coveted jobs to rich. There are some lessons to be learnt from the current functioning of the political and administrative system.

Ever heard that coveted jobs in a state being sold to the highest bidders? Looks incredible! No. It is a damn reality that happened recently when the Punjab Public Service Commission Chairman Ravinder Pal Singh Siddu, a former journalist, had developed strong panacea for striking big deals with politicians and big businessmen through favourable coverage in the press. That was his *modus operandi* which worked so well that he was soon picked up for the most prized appointment and became so powerful that no one dared to question the methods employed in collecting lakhs of rupees against a single recruitment in the government.

Naturally, such a big amount could only be paid by a top bureaucrat or a politician or a businessman. Siddu's mind was very sharp in striking such type of deals and then managing crores of rupees, which could only be the job of similar mind that could plan an elaborate system of conducting the whole operation in absolutely fool-proof manner without disturbing the basic rules and regulations of the commission for conducting various exams.

It wasn't that he was the sole person who decided everything. There was a board of members consisting of top brass who had held high positions earlier. But then with the style of functioning of the chairman they had been virtually turned into non-entity and continued to tolerate his bossism, his arbitrary behaviour, his arrogance and did not have the courage to put their foot down.

Interestingly, this high drama continued for nearly five and a half years and would have continued even longer if the Punjab government had not brought the culprit to book. The chairman himself was unaware of amount of money stashed away which was mostly in the name of his family members.

It appears that the lure of wealth had practically taken such a strong hold over him that even his shrewd mental wits failed to cope with it, and thus he was let down and fell easily into the share of the new government in Punjab when they had cleverly kept a watch when a client whom he possibly did not suspect otherwise had called on him at the appointed time to hand over half a million rupees as part of a deal, while the remaining amount would be paid at the time of issuing of the appointment letter. Thus, he ran into the clever game of the state government.

Now only time will tell about the future of this case. That the functioning of our law and society—in itself raises several eyebrows. Firstly, why should it be a time consuming process which would enable the culprit to come out as a clean person. For example, when corruption charges were levelled against former Prime Minister Narasimha Rao, he has with lapse of time turned out to be a upright person.

The children of politicians even when they commit crime come out of the prison within a period of 5 to 10 years. Even in the prison they are treated like VIPs.

Secondly, who are the people who had helped the Chairman of the Punjab Public Service Commission to amass wealth! It was of course the corrupt system of backdoor entry for the children of those who had got wealth and could therefore bid for high jobs. A large number of brilliant candidates were rejected for their only fault was they could not afford to pay such high prices.

Third, the system of corruption flourishes because of close nexus between officials and politicians. It is quite evident that had the chairman of public commission not been rewarded on the basis of his favourable covering of day-to-day performance of these politicians, he would not have got the coveted post.

Thus, there are some lessons to be learnt from the current functioning of the political and administrative system which has denied a large number of deserving candidates to get into the prized jobs. We must therefore develop a system which will select candidates on the basis of merit.

Moreover, a careful watch should be kept by social activists who are not interested in politics but are committed to social welfare, over the functioning of different bodies of the government. Here the media can play an important role.

However, from time-to-time we should create an independent body of intelligentsia to review the state of corruption in the country and their findings and recommendations should be adopted as far as possible.

This will help to eradicate this endemic disease that has taken hold of our society. India is labelled as one of the top-most corrupt countries in he world.

22. Corruption Amidst Surplus

With several states in the country entering the race of Green Revolution, there is little opportunity to market the surplus food from Punjab. With piled-up debts and pressure from creditors, there was a natural drift towards jobs mostly by the rural youth. Interestingly, corruption coincided with globalisation when a downward market trend in the farm sector began.

While Punjab was undoubtedly the first ever state in the country to earn the title of Green Revolution for several years and was the proud saviour of the country from heavy import of foodgrain which cost it dearly apart from posing a problem of uncertainty, it has unfortunately fallen into the nasty trap of scam, sex and sleaze.

One wonders whether such development is the natural consequence of having tasted a high dose of prosperity for over the years. Punjab farmers have earned undreamt income from their land which has put the state's per capita income the highest in the country and then for so long. Incidentally this was the only state in the country where the rural per capita income was higher than the urban. Indeed remarkable.

But it has lagged behind in industrialisation. Unfortunately, the average Punjabi farmer not taught thrift, saving for the rainy day, lacks in banking habit, hardly cares to put even a part of wealth he earned for future. He spent a good part of his earnings in accumulating capital assets for his land like tractor, tubewell and other items to make him more prosperous. In fact, he would even borrow heavily from banks and middlemen, unmindful of the rate of interest charged. And he did not find it difficult to honour it so long his earnings were high.

Similarly, a new class of youngsters who have emerged during the era of green revolution were even less inclined to hard work and more to luxurious living. A large number of jeeps, motor cycles, even Marutis and other vehicles were soon crowding the rural areas. Fortunately Punjab had a good network of rural roads—thanks to green revolution.

Marriages and other functions were celebrated lavishly. Thus farmers and their kith and kin spent recklessly and they failed to build up even the modest safety route in case of an emergency. They thought that such farm prosperity was a continuous cycle and they would have no longer to face difficult days.

Unfortunately they were wrong. With time several other areas in the country had also entered the race of Green Revolution and at least became self-sufficient in farm production. Thus, there was little opportunity to market all the surplus food from Punjab.

This calamity like situation had gradually started emerging in the rural areas. With piled-up debts and little chances of their good income earning and pressure from the creditors for return of borrowed money, there was a natural drift towards jobs mostly by the rural youth. But then there were few government jobs which they preferred for the chances of making extra money to compensate them for the loss their families were suffering in agriculture and allied areas.

It is here that corruption got a high fillip. Interestingly this era coincided with globalisation when a downward market trend in the farm sector had begun. That corruption had also reached its crescendo has been duly confirmed by the various enquiries that have been instituted recently. It has been beyond doubt revealed that several hundred crores of rupees have changed hands practically in every field right from the bottom of the ladder to top when the price varied with the amount of further earning potential of the job. Little surprise that today several politicians, bureaucrats and others who had exploited their position are now cooling their heels in prison.

Along with such high corruption it is but natural that moral standards also start declining. If a survey were carried to work out the link between the two evils, one would surely find a positive relationship.

It would also be idle to discuss the charges made against certain politicians for their active role in sex and sleaze as it is being done by powers in Punjab to protect their colleagues. And then chief minister is himself under the cloud which shows how things can function.

The fact that in the recent elections in Himachal Pradesh much drit was openly traded by the ruling and opposition parties to win over the support of voters. This shows the moral level to which the society has been descended when the real issues are forgotten.

What effect this is going to have in the long-run would be difficult to say, but certainly this is an unhealthy trend and should be stopped forthwith. And we should get down to discussing the real issues that face the common man. He is indeed interested in having a decent food, cloth and shelter. When the government fails to provide these basic necessities it has no right to stay in power.

And certainly the present government in Punjab which had started with a slogan of early development and which was appreciated by the voters for they had felt cheated by the previous government, but then after seeing its functioning, are finding it even less acceptable. The government has failed to formulate any worthwhile policy on agriculture, industry and core areas in infrastructure, much less implementing it. And little surprise some of them have even started looking to the governor's rule which they find worked at least in their favour.

23. Starvation Amidst Surplus

The favourable agriculture growth, instead of giving high satisfaction, has turned out to be a worrisome factor. Though we have surplus stocks, it was the poor distribution system which was a major cause for starvation deaths in Rajasthan. Apart from this, in Rajasthan, there are no proper roads, particularly in the tribal belt, the construction of which would have greatly facilitated the mobility of the local population besides ensuring smooth flow of foodgrains.

Ironically, while favourable growth of agriculture during the past over three decades, particularly in the states of north-west India should have been a cause for high satisfaction and jubilation, unfortunately it has turned out to be rather worrisome factor, more so over the last decade with a chain of bumper harvests.

In fact for the past few years our foodgrain storage position has been constantly on rise so much so that notwithstanding the recent drought situation we are still left with stocks of foodgrains which are almost three times of normal need. This, in other words, means that we have to incur a high cost on the storage of extra stocks as well as face the danger of a good part of it turning into unfit for human consumption. There is already a good amount of such stock in our godowns which besides high maintenance cost poses a high danger to public health.

Unfortunately it appears that no proper census has been carried out of this damaged stock. While it might be difficult to know its exact quantum when it is spread over a large area of the country, nevertheless it would not be advisable to keep on postponing such census, particularly when the timely elimination of damaged stock would save us from the large resources unnecessarily locked up and also more space would be available for the storage of fresh stock.

It was estimated that something like Rs. 10,000 crore were spent annually on management of vast food stocks, something like 60 million tonnes (while effectively we did not need more than 20 million tonnes at a time). This is a staggering amount which the country could ill-afford. Thus, with more effective management as well as weeding out unwanted stocks we could save a good part of this expenditure.

It is also a matter of high concern, why we are not able to make an effective use of our bulging food stocks when we are still loaded with one-third of population which is virtually half-hungry and there are also still worse pockets particularly among the remote tribal areas. Only recently it had been reported by the media about the starvation deaths among the tribals in Rajasthan.

Interestingly, the press had also pointed out gross mismanagement of food distribution system among the tribals in Rajasthan where there has been persistent drought situation for the last four years running. It was reported that in the interior tribal areas there was complete bungling of food distribution system. It was found that fair price shops—if we could call them so—received their quota of food supply only once in a month and such date was not specified before hand. While the tribal families got less ration, the inspection of books of these shopkeepers showed that they had been provided with their full quota. What happened to the unpurchased quota, one can very well imagine. In fact these very tribals, it appears, would buy the unused quota from these very shops subsequently at a much higher price.

Because of this callous food distribution system, which is so often advertised of a great help to the poorest among the poor, is a mere eyewash. Also look at the lack of any realistic approach following by the administration for creating viable employment avenues among the poor which would not only have created more purchasing capacity among these hungry people and thus help the country to get rid of these bulging food stocks, it will also at the same time help the country in creating long-term capital assets.

In Rajasthan, there are no proper roads, particularly in the tribal belt, the construction of which would have greatly facilitated the mobility of the local population as well as help in the smooth flow of foodgrains and other essential articles of daily use.

It was only in the year 2001 that while celebrating the birthday of Prime Minister Atal Behari Vajpayee an announcement was made by him to create a nationwide network of rural roads linking each and every part of the country. In fact, there was also announcement made for earmarking a sum of Rs. 60,000 crore for this gigantic programme. Many suggested in the press that this programme should be financed partly through food-for-work basis when food in place of cash was given to those employed on such construction programme.

Had this been done we would have today achieved some progress in the construction of rural roads especially in the most backward pockets as well as got rid off though partially our heavy food stocks. But then unfortunately the decision-makers generally keep themselves shut to the realities of time. While they do much of loud-talking to placate the masses, subsequently they prefer to keep silent. One wonders what would be the fate of the recently announced programme regarding the supply of potable water to all villages in the country during the next couple of years, which was also announced during the recent birthday of Prime Minister.

24. Accountable Government

The dismal picture of Indian economy bears a big contrast to the lavish expenditure incurred by political bosses on their kith and kin. The tragedy is that after committing such acts they are not answerable to anyone. Therefore, we should encourage intellectuals, NGOs and other public bodies to review the performance of politicians and bureaucrats during their tenure.

While the World Development Report paints a dismal picture of development of India among the global economies in terms of per capita income, levels of education, health, social welfare and other like indicators, it bears a big contrast to the lavish expenditure incurred by political bosses on their kith and kin. Recent example is the lavish wedding of the second daughter of Laloo Prasad Yadav, the uncrowned king of Bihar—

which incidentally happens to be among the poorest states in the country. Laloo would conveniently deny that he was milking the state treasury for his personal use. He would even add that all this was just affection and love that his people showered on him. While the estimate of this wedding goes around Rs. 100 crores, some people feel it may be far higher. And nobody would know the exact amount spent when we take into account the (forced) voluntary services rendered by the Bihar business community in making over 100 latest brands of cars available from their showrooms to receive the guests for the wedding.

Apart from that, Laloo was not satisfied unless the wedding arrangements were personally supervised by officials of the state government. Not only this. As many as half a dozen senior ministers had been drafted to manage the wedding function. They were thus given new portfolios during the marriage.

In fact, this marriage had brought the whole of Patna (read Bihar) into global limelight, which clearly shows that Bihar is no longer a poor state. But the fact remains Bihar is far lower in per capita income, literacy, health and other indicators compared to a large number of other states in the country. It is not Laloo who had displayed such extravagant expenditure, a few years back Tamil Nadu chief minister Jayalalitha had performed equally a wonderful job, perhaps even more, in the wedding of her foster son when traffic in the city of Chennai had come to a standstill for a day to allow the performance of this occasion.

However, while we blame Bihar for its poverty, what about Tamil Nadu? It ranks far higher in development indicators and is called one of the fastest progressive states of the country. It shows that the situation is same all over the country when it comes to political bosses who are experts in milking state revenues for personal affairs.

And now it is the turn of Mayawati, the new chief minister of Uttar Pradesh, who is already having plans to create memorials in the name of Ambedkar through lavishly executed memorials on prime land. Earlier, several crores were spent on the same when she was chief minister for a short time.

This money could have spent for the benefit of the poor on their education, health, employment. After all her party stands for the welfare and uplift of dalits. Unfortunately, these dalits exist only in name while the chief minister's mind is preoccupied with her own ego satisfaction in utilising state resources on areas that hardly benefit the poor. While Mahatma Gandhi often reminded politicians in particular that before they thought of spending the state resources they should closely examine how their move was actually going to benefit the poor. So their primary goal should be of wiping out poverty.

But then our leaders hardly think on Gandhi's line. They only remember the poor on the day of election when they make several promises to them but once elected these are hardly fulfilled. Rather every leader is keen to amass wealth from the state treasury.

And then the tragedy is that after committing such acts they are not answerable even to tax authority. Who is going to question Laloo for this extravagant wedding. How much amount was spent on it? What have been the sources? None would dare to do this. After some noise by the opposition parties and media the whole incident would be hushed up as it was the case with Jayalalitha.

It is time we no longer sat complacent over such unhealthy development when it is claimed that both politicians and bureaucrats are the humble servants of the people as they draw power as well as income from the people through taxes. Both politicians and bureaucrats have, over time, become the masters while it is the people who have turned humble servants. Look how an ordinary citizen is treated when he dares to call on powers that be. Not only he is denied access to a politician or a bureaucrat, he is also denied access to middle range functionaries.

Certainly this is not a healthy development that has come about during the last couple of decades when the distance between the people and the top leadership (including bureaucrats) has widened to such a level that it appears difficult to bridge unless there is a positive change in the mindset of those who govern the country.

Can we have another Mahatma Gandhi or a like leader who can bring back a healthy change in the current political scenario and remind these leaders that they are the servants of people, not the masters.

We would encourage intellectuals, NGOs and other public

bodies to review the performance of politicians and bureaucrats during their tenure so that they are told in clear terms where things had gone wrong and how these should be rectified to ensure better performance.

SECTION 9

EDUCATION

25. Rural Education Programme

India has yet not any clear policy of school education. For a proper growth education at the grass-root level such policy is needed to be developed early.

While we often boast of higher education policy, rarely we think of school education policy and possibly never of rural education policy, notwithstanding the fact that despite high urbanisation, our country even today has predominantly rural population—two-thirds of the total population. And it is here that the largest number of illiterates are to be found whose number even this day exceeds that at the time of independence. This shows how even after a period of over 50 years we have failed to achieve the most elementary input of economic and social development—literacy. Little surprise that today we happen to be the world's one of the poorest and most illiterate nations. Several developing countries which got their independence later than we did have left us far behind in the field of human development.

Even China that had started on the path of development later and was in a worse position in human development compared to us is now far better placed in basic growth indicators such as population pressure, literacy, industrialisation, skilled manpower and overall social development. It has far higher rate of literacy, especially among women while in India even today several areas continue to be obsessed with the notion that no useful purpose will be served by educating women who have by and large to manage household affairs and look after children. While much is talked about China's dictatorial administration which achieved one child family norm through instilling fear in the minds of the local population, little is appreciated of the role that literacy among women has played in this aspect. The wide population gap that existed between India and China earlier is soon on the way of closing down when we would become world's number one country in population.

Message is Clear

Thus the message is clear. In case we want to avoid further population catastrophe we must move fast enough on the road of rural literacy programme and here, especially in the sphere of female literacy, a lot of spadework is required. That a positive relation exists between female education and social development becomes evident even when we look at the experience of our own southern states which are better placed in literacy compared with the North. See what a dramatic social change has come about in Kerala where women enjoy a high rate of literacy and consequently have a say in family decision-making. While in most of the northern States such as Bihar, U.P., Rajasthan and M.P. it is the male members who have a predominantly say in family affairs.

Thus if we want to emerge from this vicious circle of population and poverty—both are so closely interrelated—high priority should be given to rural education.

So far, with our bias for higher education we have failed to provide sufficient funds as well as attention to rural education. It is well known that benefits of higher education have only gone to a small segment of the population, mainly the urban elite. Even in school education much attention has been paid to urban schools. In rural education programme we have imposed school curriculum irrespective of whether it suits the needs of rural children who live under a totally different environment. Equally there has been a tendency to employ urban trained teachers to man rural schools who generally hail from neighbouring towns and have little interest in rural schools.

Uninteresting Approach

With such a system how can we expect rural children to take interest in their education? While we attribute the high dropout rates from rural schools to all sorts of flimsy excuses like illiterate parents who are not in favour of getting their children educated as well as family compulsions, we rarely bother to get down to the root cause of the problem which is clearly the uninteresting approach adopted to educate these children with city-based books and teachers. Both have been a big failure.

Every State should therefore commit a major portion of its education budget to rural education instead of diverting it for higher education; in fact, a good part of the latter can be effectively delivered by the private sector as has been the experience of the southern states. For training rural teachers special institutes should be set-up where they are provided intensive training in the new system of rural education. It would be appropriate that in future such teachers have also rural moorings as they would then be more committed to rural education than their urban counterparts.

Much effort should go in for preparing new courses relevant to rural environments. While we have a national body like the NCERT, very little effort has been made by this body in the area of rural education. In fact, in its high profile programmes little has been done to draft textbooks that would suit the needs of rural children where a lot of effort is needed to understand their special needs and interest. Here individual interest of both boys and girls as well as of the community would have to be kept in view. Their special needs for agriculture, environment, vocational and allied courses would have to be dovetailed into these courses. Girls should have exposure to courses that are relevant to them.

Also we have hitherto made little attempt in providing infrastructure for delivering rural education. Several areas yet do not have proper school buildings and where these exist they are not well maintained. Now we have panchayats practically in all villages; these bodies should be made responsible for construction as well as maintenance of school buildings, for which sufficient funds should be provided. Also why should the rural education be under the charge of the District Education Officer whose staff rarely visit these schools much less the DEO? We should discard this bureaucratic system and instead ensure effective decentralisation and management of the rural education programme. Let us strengthen panchayats in this respect which should be able to deliver the goods more effectively.

Thus a meaningful rural education programme and its effective implementation would help wipe out the high illiteracy in the country, especially among women.

26. Address Language Barrier

Unlike the migrant labour the situation for migrant educated people from Bimaru states is not quite encouraging for the basic reason that this educated manpower neither has the skill required nor they are in a position to pick it up because of their language barrier. In the interest of youth in Hindi states it would be advisable to expose them to English language in a meaningful manner.

While hitherto we have often highlighted the problem of the migrant labour from the Bimaru states (Bihar, Madhya Pradesh, Rajasthan, Uttar Pradesh) and that most of this labour has settled in the north-eastern area (Punjab, Haryana, Chandigarh and Delhi especially) where there are employment opportunities, we have not brought out another peculiar phenomenon that has been going on simultaneously—the migration of the educated unemployed from these very states where their number has fast picked up recently.

In fact, in the Union Territory of Chandigarh itself while around two-third of the total migrant population comprises of labourers from these states, which has almost choked its periphery and destroyed much of the greenery, there has also been a rising trend of the migration of the educated unemployed from the Bimaru states. This becomes obvious from the registers maintained by the city's employment exchanges.

It obviously shows that these states have failed to create opportunities for their educated manpower due to the slow pace of development, when it is well-known that it is mostly the private sector that has the potential to create large employment avenues especially for the educated as the government sector has its limitations. So is true about the public sector, where the government's disinvestment policy has only worsened the situation. While structural reforms and globalisation were expected to bring about a large measure of relief in the employment scenario, that unfortunately has not happened as fresh activities under their functioning have concentrated only on selected areas which are already developed or has holds development potential. Unfortunately Bimaru states have neither. Thus not many private firms have found it profitable to invest there.

Due to lack of industrialisation, there is a high growth in unemployment rate in these states. In other words, while universities in these states have been churning out graduates and even post-graduates in record number, they have only added to the unemployment stream where most of them, like illiterate workers, have been forced to try their luck in those very states where the migrant labour has been crowding.

But unlike the migrant labour the situation for educated people is not quite encouraging for the basic reason that this educated manpower neither has the skill required to qualify for a good job nor they are in a position to pick it up because of their language barrier.

Unfortunately whatever English is taught to them in schools is done in a slipshod manner by teachers who themselves are not qualified. Thus, the end result is that they do not possess even the minimum working knowledge of English. In other words, the excessive dependence on Hindi has cost them dear and they find it difficult to qualify even for the lowest possible job, which though does not require much knowledge of English at least expects working background. Little surprise therefore that even post-graduate students from these states face difficulty in finding a job.

This is the major problem that a student from these areas had to face. He has hardly been made to realise that though Hindi is the national language it is not quite popular. In fact, all the modern offices in the country use only English. Even in government offices in most of the states as well as in Centre while Hindi may be used to indicate that it is the national language, much of the work is done in English.

In south the situation is still more difficult. And in a state like Tamil Nadu one would be a stranger if he communicated in Hindi as most of them use either local language or English. This is the primary reason that rarely a person from the Bimaru states would go down to south India for employment. The same is true in case of North-East, where one has to speak either the tribal language or English barring of course some areas here and there.

The Hindi medium teaching has deprived the students in picking up modern areas of communication like information technology which enjoys fast expanding market. Because of the language handicap they have concentrated mostly in learning courses in arts and very few have opted for professional courses. Thus, they have a long way to go to compete with students from other universities and unless they take up seriously learning English they would remain cut-off from the mainstream.

It also needs to be understood that English is no longer the colonial language but it is universally accepted and spoken language. Even in those lands where the national language rules supreme like Japan and China it is English which is finding large acceptance.

On the other hand, in our country we still continue to be carried by the false notion that English is a foreign language, which was imposed on us by the Britishers.

In our own country states that enjoy higher rate of industrialisation as well as of services are invariable those where English has gained a considerable success. Their counterpart Hindi states have been left far behind. And this phenomenon has been all the more apparent under recent globalisation when opportunities in the Hindi-patronising states have failed to grow anywhere near the states using English.

Even the flow of foreign capital and technology has failed to make any significant entry into the Bimaru states while the story is different in other states, especially in the southern and western states.

So the lesson is apparent. In the interest of youth in Hindi states who at the end of their education are thrown into the job market in other states, it would be advisable to expose them to English language in a meaningful manner so that they are able to compete effectively with their counterparts from other states.

And ultimately this tradition would also help rapid development of these very states when the educated youth, instead of seeking employment avenues in other states, would find ample opportunities within their own states.

27. Attention not Paid to Quality

Much of the decline in education standard has emerged after we started multiplying universities and colleges without bothering about the quality of education. Sadly after setting up a number of commissions to reform the system of education we are still nowhere near a uniform national educational policy in the country.

One is appalled at looking into the quality of products churned out by most of our universities. There was a time when with around a dozen or so universities in the whole country which included the present Pakistan and Bangladesh, even Sri Lanka, produced much better products, despite the fact that several areas in the country could not have access to such education. Students had better grasp over subjects and it was particularly in English they fared far better than does the present generation emerging from over 200 universities and several thousands of colleges.

With fast multiplication of universities the quality of our education has declined. The modern system of education is just confined to microscopic minority—mainly the upper layer of the society—while the vast number has a poor grasp of modern development in science and technology and several other areas.

Most of students approach under the current system is confined to cheap text books and notes prepared by their teachers, most of which rarely revised. Rarely they care to read the prescribed texts. Not only this, quite a few teachers may not even be aware of them and much less talk of consulting articles in the scholarly journals.

Rarely one finds them sitting in the library. When this is the case with teachers how do you expect students to visit library. Several teachers are occupied with private tuitions which brings them handsome income notwithstanding the fact the current pay scales of college and university teachers are quite liberal much out of proportion with the employees in private and government organisations. So to be a teacher is a big blessing. The whole system of education has turned out to be corrupt and needs to be examined closely by another education commission.

At the same time, it is not that all universities have got into such mire. There are yet very good universities where high standards of education continue to be maintained but they are like a small oasis in a desert. On the whole, most of our universities and colleges are in bad shape and the nation spends on them several hundred crores of rupees in the name of education.

Much of this decline in education standard has emerged after we started multiplying universities and colleges without bothering about the quality of education. The situation is worst in those areas where the local language has been blindly replaced by English. The worst culprits here are the Hindi states going under the nomenclature of Bimaru. They are indeed sick states where education needs to be structurally reformed. Unfortunately these states have the largest number of universities in the country where they excel in the delivery of courses in Hindi only and have practically banished English from their institutions and students find it very comfortable in expressing in their own language and secure very high marks. While Japan had adopted the local language for teaching in their institutions, it was only done after the western text books were translated appropriately in the local language by committed scholars. Not only this. The translated texts were often exposed to rigid scrutiny and any fault discovered was corrected in time and in fact these books were adopted only after the administration was fully satisfied with the quality. It was also possible to do this because Japan did not face the problem of multiple languages like India.

Lately, Japan too has recognised the fact that despite such bias for the local language they were yet far behind the western countries. This deficiency is now gradually being rectified by the larger use of English.

In fact, Japan would be far ahead of us in English, while only a few years back an average Indian felt quite comfortable in English in foreign countries while participating in seminars and other programmes. Thanks to the muddled language policy in India, neither we have been able to develop the national language Hindi nor English, notwithstanding the fact that English is no longer the language of the Englishman alone, it is the universal language for communication and business. Even the post-graduate students from the Hindi speaking states are afraid of visiting some places within the country for they would not feel comfortable with the knowledge of Hindi alone.

Unfortunately even the southern states, which at one time boasted their higher grasp over English and whose products would find top jobs under the British administration, are now no longer better than their Hindi-speaking counterparts. The southern states had been gradually losing their presence in these top services basically because they had become excessive lover of the local language like north Indians. When English was the only language for national unity and administration when we were able to produce the best civil servants (ICS) and other Asian countries looked at us with jealously, now the situation is so very different. Many countries have overtaken us in business and trade where the neglect of English has been one principle factor.

Indeed at one time the universities of Madras, Bombay, Calcutta and Allahabad produced the finest administrators, academicians, scholars, politicians, judicial luminaries, scientists—in fact their students excelled well in one or the other field. Today all these universities are facing one or the other crises and their teaching and research standards have gone down.

There are of course some universities in English dominating areas like Delhi, Chandigarh and Institutes of Technology and Management where English is still supreme and these institutions have also done well. In fact, in the central services the products of these universities and national institutes have found the maximum entry. They have also done well in global placements and are preferred for the jobs advertised through the UPSC.

We should realise the damage we have done by neglecting English and giving upper hand to a host of local languages where we have by and large failed in delivering quality education and building some uniform system of administration and employment in the country. Certainly students from the

Bimaru states would be misfit outside their states. Such examples are found in abundance when graduates and post-graduates from these universities who are registered with employment exchanges are not able to find job even after waiting long.

We should seriously think over the whole matter of education and move with the globalisation trend where English is must for everyone. Sadly even after so many years of independence and setting up a number of commissions to reform the system of education in the country and holding seminars, conferences and programmes we are still nowhere near a uniform national educational policy.

In fact any uniformity in education system cannot be possible unless we have some link language which is nationally acceptable. So long as Hindi does not come to this level it would be best to give preference to English.

28. Neglecting Education of the Poor

For several years rural education received low priority in our agenda. In the larger interest of the country we have to develop a system of education both at school and higher level that fits the needs of the country and only in this way we would be able to derive the maximum benefit in line with our priorities.

One of the tragedies with this country is that while we promise, commit ourselves en block—interestingly it is only here that all political parties combine together, show absolute solidarity, but when it comes to achieve the goal we all very conveniently back away. It is the same fate that has met our education system. More than half a century ago, just after achieving independence, we made a firm commitment cutting across all political parties, that by the year 2000 the country would be absolutely free from illiteracy when it would have hundred per cent literate population.

The reality on the other hand has been that while we have crossed 2000 the situation of literacy in the country has hardly changed, the number of illiterates in the country are yet close to they were in 1950!

On the other hand, resources earmarked for education have been by and large diverted to supporting a chain of universities and higher institutions of learning. In 1950, the country had 27 universities, the number equivalent to what we have today in the state of Maharashtra alone, and it is UP (of course including Uttaranchal) which has the highest number of universities in the country and simultaneously it is this very state (particularly its vast eastern belt) which has the maximum number of illiterates in the country.

Thus within a short span of couple of decades, there was virtual spree for creating new universities which were likened to new temples by Pandit Nehru and every chief minister irrespective of the party he belonged was keen to add more and more of these new temples to his state kitty. Thus the number of universities and higher institutes that a state possessed became a symbol of prestige.

And in this rat race of creating new universities and higher institutes we completely lost sight of what we had vowed to achieve. Rural education for several years occupied low priority in our agenda. In fact, the same was true of rural development itself which for years remained a neglected area. Unfortunately our planners who hailed from urban areas and several of them being educated in foreign universities were anxious to develop urban areas thinking that if these developed the rural areas would automatically pick up. Unfortunately that was not so and could not be by any stretch of imagination. Thus, there was a big divide between rural and urban development. Over years this dischotomy instead of narrowing down has widened further and thus most of the earlier economic development benefited the urban society—the middle class population mainly and there was utter neglect of their poor cousins staying in rural areas. In fact better-off members from rural areas gradually shifted to urban destinations, thus creating further divide between rural and urban areas.

Soon we had to suffer from the adverse consequences of such neglect of education in rural areas. That there exists direct link between education and development of human resources is well-known and is amply justified from the experience of other countries. The present developed economies also faced at one time the situation that we faced at the time of independence with a large percentage of illiterate population. However, these countries were shrewd enough to realise the long-term benefit of literacy and thus accorded the foremost priority in educating their population irrespective of their place of residence.

In fact special efforts were made to educate population in rural areas with simple courses that met their needs. Their curriculum was developed keeping in view special needs of such population and little surprise that soon education had made a deep dent and paid a rich dividend in their all round development. The divide that earlier existed between rural and urban areas was soon bridged and the rural population began to play an important role in their nation-building programmes, supplied the labour force that their industries needed and helped in laying the foundation of communication network.

Thus instead there occurring exodus to urban areas like the one we have witnessed during the past 50 years, most of their rural areas themselves slowly got urbanised and thus all those facilities that are an integral part of urban living were available in rural areas. Thus there was complete transformation of rural areas. In fact members of higher income of population preferred to stay in the quiet and serene surrounding of rural areas which enjoyed all the modern facilities. Even in our country we have witnessed the healthy impact of the spread of literacy in rural areas. We have before us the example of the Kerala in the south where there is almost cent per cent literacy including among women.

It is in this state that now it is women who take most of the decisions in domestic matters, including number of children to be had and other important family matters. This has helped the state to have the best family norm of one child family. This state is also on the top of women and children health care and welfare.

On the other hand, take the case of so-called Bimaru states of Bihar, Madhya Pradesh, UP, and Rajasthan which are crowd with a very large population of illiterates—in fact the largest concentrate of illiterates is to be found here and the worst thing is that the status that women enjoyed here is deplorable with a heavy load of children along with poor economic development.

Instead of spending on literacy our country has been keen to spread family planning programme. This shows that without literacy and social development especially among women the family planning programme in itself would fail to transform the thinking of the population.

It is not only that we have bungled in our educational programme, we have also not tried to reorient our higher education, which as mentioned above has received the highest attention, in accordance with the needs of the country. While we have been spending our scarce resources liberally on the education of doctors or other experts where the courses are at par with foreign universities, they are quite reluctant to serve in rural areas.

The result is that most of them, at least till recently, migrated to developed countries in the West where they needed their services. But then at what cost? While the country makes costly investment in training these young people it fails to derive the benefit, instead this system has helped other countries to derive the maximum benefit. This shows how sticking to the elitist courses failed to meet the needs of rural population. We have done great damage to our own country, when simple courses keeping in view the needs of the rural population could have created an alternative cadre of rural doctors which could have served the needs of the population in a better way. And that exactly is what our neighbour China did. They created a cadre of so-called 'barefoot doctors' with far less investment and tremendous saving in time on their education and training and such paramedical staff has served well the needs of the rural population who needed care generally for elementary ailments. And since most of these doctors had their roots in rural areas they were easy to contact and thus most of the ailments of rural people were treated. This also helped to reduce pressure on urban hospitals and clinics. Similar is the case with school education. We still stick to urban-biased text books which fit little to the needs and interest of rural children. Even teachers are mostly from urban areas who have little interest in rural education. Little surprise that there are large dropouts in school education and thus hardly any worthwhile system of rural education has developed hitherto. All these programmes need to be closely looked into and unless made an integral part of rural needs they will fail to serve their purpose.

Thus in the larger interest of the country we have to develop a system of education both at school and higher level that fits into the needs of the country and only in this way we would be able to derive the maximum benefit in line with our priorities.

While the western brand of education has its important place in our development, but at the same time we should not close our eyes to hard realities of this country where social ethos and local problems are so very different from those found in advanced countries. We have yet to close this gap before we could synthesis ourselves with the global economy. Thus, there is very justification in developing our own system of education, health, social life, industry, agriculture and commerce and gradually make it an integral part of global socio-economic development.

Briefly, the lop-sided programme that we have developed over the past more than half a century tells how badly we have failed to develop alternative indigenous brand of education as well as growth model which was capable of putting the economy on a stable footing and better serve the needs of our population.

9

Summing Up : Balanced Rural-Urban Development

"The challenge before all of us is to collectively rise to the task ahead of us in terms of increasing rural incomes, removing poverty and giving control to local levels to plan for themselves thereby strengthening the democratic process . . ."

—*Dr. Manmohan Singh*

RURAL DEVELOPMENT PROGRAMMES : HIGHLIGHTS

Promoting Self-Employment in Rural Areas

- ☐ Swarnajayanti Gram Swarozgar Yojana (SGSY) aiming at promoting self-employment of the rural poor launched on 1st April, 1999 with emphasis on organising the rural poor into Self-Help Groups (SHGs) and ensuring their capacity building, training, economic assistance, marketing and related infrastructure.
- ☐ Since inception 17.73 lakh SHGs formed. Out of 46.44 lakh Swarozgaris assisted till March 2004, 21 lakh Swarozgaris were SCs/STs and about 21 lakh were women.

Ensuring Food Security and Gainful Employment

- Sampoorn Grameen Rozgar Yojana (SGRY), with an annual outlay of Rs. 10,000 crore, aims at providing wage employment to women, SCs/STs and parents of children withdrawn from hazardous occupations.
- A minimum of 5 kg. of foodgrains is provided in addition to cash payment as wages to the poor through creation of durable community assets.
- So far 221.44 crore mandays generated.

Strengthening Rural Infrastructure

- Pradhan Mantri Gram Sadak Yojana (PMGSY), aims at connecting all unconnected rural habitations (around 1.70 lakh) with a population of 500 or above with all-weather roads.
- Proposals for 35,305 road works covering 94,829 kms. estimated to cost Rs. 14,715 crore have been cleared.
- Habitations with 1000+ population in 15 States will be provided connectivity with the completion of projects approval.

Shelter for All

- Indira Awaas Yojana (IAY) seeks to provide assistance for construction of houses to BPL rural households, SCs/STs and freed bonded labour.
- About 1.14 crore houses constructed involving an expenditure of Rs. 20,000 crore.
- About 15 lakh houses are constructed every year under IAY.

Potable Drinking Water for All

- 99.58% rural habitations have already got access to safe drinking water.
- A community-based rural water supply programme 'Swajaldhara' launched in December 2002. Under 'Swajaldhara' 10% capital cost and full operation and maintenance cost is borne by users.
- Special efforts made to conserve water sources and to provide safe drinking water in rural habitations

affected by water quality having fluorosis, arsenic, salinity and iron in excess.

Rejuvenating Wastelands/Degraded Lands

- ☐ A quantum jump in the budget provision from Rs. 324 crore in 1999-2000 to Rs. 1,261 crore in the current year.
- ☐ Projects covering an area of 194.19 lakh hectares taken up from 1.4.1995 to March 2004.
- ☐ Under the new initiative 'Hariyali' a greater role for Panchayats has been envisaged.

Promoting Cleanliness and Hygiene in Rural Areas

- ☐ Total Sanitation Campaign with an outlay of Rs. 3,750 crore is being implemented in 398 districts.
- ☐ Nirmal Gram Puruskar for achieving 100% open defecation-free environment launched on 2nd October 2003 to motivate the Panchayati Raj institutions.
- ☐ So far 8.7 million household toilets constructed. Rs. 195 crore contributed by people.

TOWARDS BALANCED RURAL-URBAN DEVELOPMENT

By mapping the last more than a decade's experience, it is quite clear that benefits of globalization and open economy introduced in 1991 have almost exclusively gone over to the urban areas and the rural areas have got either negative or marginal benefits from such development.

Thus, it has left a big gap between rural-urban development which needs to be closed down early. Interestingly while the Planning Commission has been often proclaiming that gains from development would be equally divided between these two sectors, it has in reality not happening. It also appears that lately the role of Planning Commission, after India's surrender to globalised economy, has been reduced to that of secondary importance. At least that is what is obvious from recent developments.

It is therefore also time that the functioning of this august body was put under close scrutiny and whatever loopholes found should be dealt with sternly. Now with the induction of Montek Ahluwalia an ace planner who has held senior positions both within this country as well as in the UN, as its Deputy Chairman, things would move at a fast pace and the functioning of the Commission would be revamped.

Also the national budget presented recently in the Parliament speaks high of introducing measures that would change the rural scenario during the tenure of the present government.

Employment

As it has been highlighted earlier, the country has to accord a high priority to rural employment which has failed to pick-up since the introduction of globalisation. The rural poverty as well as unemployment have to be tackled almost at war footing and radical policy framework should be attempted to achieve it.

Often it is observed that once the viable employment opportunities are created on sustainable basis, these do bring about several positive gains including children going regularly to school and taking good interest in studies. In fact now with eight-year compulsory schooling, which is also the major objective of the present government, absence of children from school or their being withdrawn by their family to earn extra income to keep the spectre of hunger away from their door, would certainly make a big mockery of this ambitious programme.

So to achieve this goal, which is also highly meaningful, we should first of all ensure that at least one person from each rural family is employed on a gainful job for the whole year and not for a part of the year as it has been suggested by the present government. That would have no meaning as it would fail to serve its purpose.

But then the question arises, where are the jobs? Agreed. It would take time to create such large-scale jobs particularly for a population which is mostly illiterate and lacks in skills. It is here that the programme of rural capital formation in key areas of rural development comes to rescue.

There is the programme of rural communications which has a large absorbing capacity of the unskilled labour. It would have to be tapped with full vigour.

For an effective tapping of rural programmes, both Central Government and Panchayats should join hands. In fact hitherto we have far less tapped the contribution of Panchayats which though have their feet deeply planted in the rural areas. No other rural agency has this advantage. Further they are well established and by now got over their initial handicaps. Thus, they are the best source to watch the interest of rural population.

Further these programmes would not only create viable job opportunities, these would equally help to make productive use of surplus food in the country for feeding the semi-starved people who would now be in a position to purchase their needs from the fair price shops.

Since there is a big backlog in rural communication programme, it could well sustain a long time employment programme. All that is required is that it should be wisely tapped and closely watched at various levels to weed out possible corruption and misuse of funds. That's also one of the reasons why there should be close involvement of Panchayats in this programme; it would reduce misutilisation of huge funds that would be flowing into these programmes. Also NGOs which are already involved in rural development programmes and have a fair track record of their functioning would be a great help in keeping a close watch on these programmes.

Much would of course be gained through experience. In any case too much of interference by the bureaucracy, which earlier had resulted in the misuse of funds, should be avoided.

There should also be a time limit for the completion of different programmes for too much delay in their execution would be harmful for the economy. Also these programmes should be periodically reviewed and loopholes found corrected.

Water Supply

Apart from roads and other communication programmes, rural water supply is a major project which calls for early action. Still a large part of the rural areas is not linked with potable drinking water with the result people are forced to drink whatever water is available and thus often suffer from various diseases which take a heavy toll of the population.

It is also found that while agriculture continues to occupy a very important place in our rural economy and on it depends almost the entire rural population, it continues to face irrigation problem. Particularly in the rain-scarce areas of north, north-west and central India. While we had a good cycle of rainfall since globalisation, the situation this year appears to be uncomfortable when a good part of the country appears to be deprived of rainfall which spells difficult days for the farmers and the country. It would certainly affect our economy and particularly agriculture.

It is irony that while eastern and north-eastern parts of the country get flooded every year through excessive rainfall and their rivers overflow and soon a large quantity of their precious water gets emptied in Bay of Bengal, several parts of the country on the other hand cry for water. How could we solve this delicate situation? In other words, how we could link rivers so that at least a part of the overflowing water from the eastern and north-eastern rivers was made available to water hungry areas.

Our experts should closely examine this issue. If we succeed even partially to met the demand of water scarce areas, which would be a great relief. Also as rightly done by the present government, the rain water harvesting is now onwards going to be encouraged in a big way in dry areas through the creation of watershed irrigation facilities at different points. It would help the storage of rain water in different needy areas which would thus help the utilisation of water for different needs throughout the year. At present most of the rain water is allowed to flow down to rivers and not used to agriculture.

Thus, water has a vital role to play and it calls for a close attention at different points. If it was properly done, the unfortunate interstate river disputes would not arise which at present make a sad reading.

It is said that at present over 90 per cent of our river water is allowed to be emptied in oceans. If a part of it could be harnessed and made available for use it would be a great blessing for scarcity areas. The government should give a close attention to this problem, which would make a major contribution to rural development.

Similarly, several other issues have arisen during the course of this attempt which also need to be paid due attention.

We have also pointed out that while the rural development is now the major area of attention, but then not an exclusive area. The country has made such a good progress in urban industrialisation, growth of service sector, introduction of new technology in almost all areas and future also holds a good attention for their development and several other areas.

So appropriate attention should continue to be paid to urban development, globalisation and market economy. In fact, sooner we are able to change the rural scenario and bring it close to the urban areas, larger chances would be there for the flow of foreign investment and technology to the rural areas as well.

In fact, through small industry programme, which also occupies a good part of attention under CMP, we should encourage such investment particularly in areas like agri-industries, diversification of crops, etc.

Thus by careful planning of programmes of rural development and their appropriate execution we would certainly be able to bring the neglected population of villages in the mainstream of the urban life, ultimately resulting in a balanced rural-urban development.

BOOKS BY DR. V.S. MAHAJAN

1. Planning, Development and Economic Policy (1973 & 1982)
2. Socialistic Pattern in India : An Assessment (1973)
3. Current International Economic Problems (1973)
4. Development Planning, Lessons from Japanese Model (1976)
5. Recent Issues in International Finance and Development (1977)
6. Towards a Theory of Economic Development (1978)
7. Economic Development with Special Reference to Problems of Underdeveloped Countries (1982)
8. Indian Economy and Regional Development (1982)
9. Planning and Socialistic Transformation of Indian Economy (1982)
10. Economic Development of India (1983)
11. Growth of Agriculture and Industry in India (1983)
12. Studies in Indian Economy (edited) (1983)
13. Energy Development in India (edited) (1983)
14. Recent Development in Indian Economy (1984)
15. Growth of Oilseeds and Allied Industries in India (1984)
16. Studies in Indian Agriculture and Rural Development (edited) (1986)
17. Studies in Industrial Economy of India (edited) (1987)
18. Emerging Pattern of North Eastern Economy (edited) (1987)
19. Economic Development of Border States of India (edited) (1988)
20. Studies in Indian Planning (edited) (1988)
21. Women's Contribution to Indian Economic and Social Development (edited) (1989)
22. Studies in Indian Banking and Finance (two volumes) (edited) (1989)
23. Planning of Developing Economies (1990)

24. Management of Indian Economy (edited) (1990)
25. International Economy : Recent Developments and Future Prospects (edited) (1990)
26. Agriculture and Rural Economy in India (1990)
27. Transport Planning, Policy and Development (edited) (1991)
28. Studies in Energy and Economic Development (edited) (1991)
29. Environment Planning, Machinery and Management (edited) (1991)
30. Social, Economic and Political Development in India (1991)
31. National Energy : Policy, Crisis and Growth (edited) (1991)
32. India's Foreign Trade and Balance of Payments (edited) (1992)
33. Indian Economy Towards 2000 A.D. (1992)
34. Environment Protection : Challenges and Issues (edited) (1993)
35. Employment Through Rural Development : Towards Sustainability (edited) (1993)
36. Manmohan's India and Other Current Writings (1994)
37. Agriculture, Rural Development and Panchayati Raj (Two Volumes) (edited) (1996)
38. Political Economy of Reforms and Liberalisation (Two Volumes) (edited) (1997)

Index